CONTENTS

DAVID ROLLO
LOCAL HERO

Best Wishes

Dave Rollo

ANDREW ARBUCKLE

First published in Great Britain in 2016
by Andrew Arbuckle

ISBN: 978-0-9928090-2-7

British Library Cataloguing-in-Publication Data
A catalogue record for this book is available on request from the
British Library.

Designed and typeset by Polaris Publishing, Edinburgh
www.polarispublishing.com

Printed in Great Britain by J Thomson, Printers, Glasgow

For Jessica, Archie and Emma

INTRODUCTION

IN THE 1960s, Dave Rollo played for Scotland forty times equalling the then record number of caps for a rugby player. He was always a distinctive player on the field of play, not just because his socks were always around his ankles, but by his amazing ability to emerge from mauls, ball in hand, leading the charge upfield.

Playing in an amateur era, he would play for Scotland on a Saturday afternoon in front of a vast crowd and the next morning be back feeding his sheep or cattle on the family farm.

Over three decades of playing, Dave was a one club man and he would often turn out for the Howe of Fife team just days after playing for one of the big invitational teams such as the Barbarians or the Co-optimists.

He trained once per week with his clubmates and backed this up by his own routines at home with a section of the road outside the farm being used for his running. There being no gymnasium for weight training, he spent days lifting sacks of grain and potatoes to help build up the muscles he needed for his tussles in the front row of the scrum.

Throughout his thirty years in the physical game of rugby, he was only once cautioned by a referee for his behaviour and this was for a vigorous hand off and not, as the official saw it, a rabbit punch.

While playing hard, Dave and his colleagues also enjoyed lots of escapades and high jinks although this did, on one occasion, see him appear in the local magistrates' court charged with driving away the team bus without permission. His team mates had no complaints about his driving and neither did they ever find fault with the quality of his rugby.

Commentators would invariably include him in their selected, "Best ever player lists" such was his imposing presence on the field and his influence in the scrum.

CHAPTER ONE

LIFE WITH THE LIONS

THE GROUND UNDER his feet was hard. The deep red dusty soil showed through the patches of grass on the pitch while the sun shone relentlessly down from a clear blue sky as the British Lions rugby team stepped out into the arena. For David Miller Durie Rollo, this was the culmination of his rugby career.

Far behind him were his schoolboy, football playing days and his late entry into picking up the oval ball. Not so far behind him was the honour of being the first Howe of Fife player to be picked to play for Scotland. Now in the bright red Lions jersey, he was playing for one of the most famous rugby teams in the world.

The British & Irish Lions, to give them their full title, are the pick of four countries – Scotland, England, Wales and Ireland. Towards the end of the Five Nations tournament, which also includes France, Dave had been quietly informed his name was in the frame for the tour. Also, off the record, he was asked if he would be available if selected. Faced with every rugby player's dream, he replied, "Yes."

Now in the thin air in Bulawayo, the second largest city in Zimbabwe which lies some 4,500 feet above sea level, the 1962 British Lions team was about to be put to the test. Although the month of May marks the start of the winter season in the southern hemisphere, the temperature in the city was well above 20 degrees Centigrade for most of the day and there had been little rainfall to dampen the hard ground.

These were the playing conditions and this was the starting point of a tour which would last for some 12 weeks. It would involve some 25 games culminating in four Test matches against South Africa. The tour time might have been well below the eighteen months the first tourists from the Home Nations took on for their inaugural visit to New Zealand in 1888 but it was also the last lengthy Lions tour. Since then improvements in air travel have given more flexibility and have drastically cut down the need for extended trips abroad.

Bulawayo at high altitude was deliberately chosen as the starting point for the 1962 Lions tour as the playing conditions they would experience there would be replicated time and again as the tour progressed into South Africa.

The actual letter inviting Dave to join the tour arrived at his Wester Forret farm in Fife on 26th March 1962. While it contained tremendous news, it did cause concern in the Rollo household on two fronts.

Dave and his wife Jean had recently become the extremely proud parents of Pat. Their daughter was less than three months old when the invitation letter popped through the farmhouse door. Leaving his wife and their small child was a big concern for Dave. Jean solved the dilemma by pointing out that the invitation to become a British Lion was a 'once in four years' opportunity and as Dave would be 32 years old when the next Lions tour was scheduled, he might then be considered to be too old.

That still left the other problem of whether the family farm could do without a key member of its workforce. Dave and his brother Ian were very much hands-on farmers and the departure from the 400 plus acre unit for three and a half months from 10th May to 30th August could have created problems in ensuring the farm work was carried out timeously.

However, with the busy spring sowing period completed and harvesting not normally getting underway until September, Ian gave his consent saying he would manage the farm by himself in the interim period. It was perhaps not so much giving consent, more of a deal whereby Ian could follow his own sport – curling – in winter by which time Dave would be at home.

The domestic hurdles cleared, it was down to preparing for the tour itself. The first step for the thirty top players drawn from the four Home Countries saw them gather in London where they met old friends and adversaries, all of whom now bonded together under the British Lions banner.

The country with the largest representation on the 1962 Lions tour was Wales with nine players going on tour while England had eight, Ireland seven and Scotland six.

Being a selector for a Lions tour has always been a poisoned chalice as over every Five Nations campaign each home country's supporters manage to build up a jaundiced view of players from the other parts of the United Kingdom but this was, in players chosen, a very equable group. This division was demonstrated later in the tour when the four nations took part in an informal seven-a-side tournament.

Six Scots and an Irishman in a Sevens Tournament on a Lions Tour in Durban.
Back row: John Douglas, Mike Campbell-Lamerton, Dave, Ronnie Cowan.
Front row: Gordon Waddell, Irishman Harry McGibbon, Arthur Smith.

Apart from Dave Rollo, the Scots in the party were Arthur Smith, Ronnie Cowan, John Douglas, Mike Campbell-Lamerton and Gordon Waddell. The Lions players, who were all amateurs and included members of the Armed Forces alongside teachers, or schoolmasters as they were called, bankers and factory workers, were told they would get fifty shillings (£2.50) per day pocket or spending money.

As it turned out, this cash was hardly needed as the players received tremendous hospitality wherever they went with many invitations out for meals and visits to tourist attractions coming from expats and rugby supporters. A number of the players smoked. Not just the odd celebratory cigar but also in that era where the health hazards from smoking were not fully understood and there was a glamour image associated with smoking, they puffed away on cigarettes. These were freely available in the hotels in which they stayed.

Possibly conscious of the small financial reward the players were receiving, the tour organisers ensured each player was provided with two free tickets for every match. These became an informal currency often being given to friends in exchange for hospitality.

The Lions management also took care of any presents the players bought and sent the gifts back to the United Kingdom as the tour progressed rather than leaving the players with having to deal with ever increasing piles of baggage.

The London preparation period saw team members receive their kit which in those days consisted of two blazers, one for wearing during the day and the other, a double breasted effort for evening wear to which were added two pairs of flannels. Responsibility for shoes was left to the players but ties with the Lion's head motif were provided as was all the playing kit which had been supplied by the four Home Unions. In the late nineteenth and early twentieth century, composite touring teams representing the four Home Nations were called after the team captain. But after the Lion's head emblem first appeared in 1924 as a logo all future teams were christened 'The Lions' or more lengthily and correctly 'The British & Irish Lions'.

The blazers and flannels provided a problem for Dave as he was a regular wearer of the kilt and his ancient Hunting MacIntosh kilt went with him whenever he was representing his country – be it Scotland or with the British Lions. This particular tartan was that of Dave's grandmother's family and he had been brought up to wear a kilt from an early age believing that the wearing of the national garment should be supported.

The bright red Lions tops, which are so associated with the Lions, first appeared in 1950. Prior to that, various team colours had been used by the touring teams. On the Lions shirt that Dave was given, the number 23 was emblazoned on the back. Traditionally the Lions tourists play with the same number throughout their tour as opposed to modern practice where numbers are allocated according to playing position on the field.

With the pre-tour practicalities over, it was down to a week of hard training at Eastbourne on the south coast of England for the 1962 tourists. This was the same location that their predecessors in the 1955 Lions tour had been put through their paces. It was also the chosen final training area for UK athletes, including Scotsman Eric Liddell, in their preparation for the Paris Olympics in 1924.

For the Lions, the training programme was tough with up to seven hours per day practising moves, going over tactics and generally getting their fitness levels up to the top level. Unlike today where coaching is far more specialised, the training routines were largely taken by the team manager and the captain.

Off the pitch the regime was strict with alcohol being forbidden – but in compensation, there was always loads of good quality food.

A brief return visit to London included an official visit to South Africa House where the team was introduced to the South African Ambassador. This was followed by an organised trip to the theatre where a diplomat had decided the players would benefit from seeing a musical highlighting the differences between "black South Africa" and "white South Africa" which the team would encounter on their travels. While some of the Scottish contingent, including Dave, had previously travelled in South Africa and had witnessed the segregation of the people, for the majority of the travellers this separation of black and white members of the human race would be a new and strange experience.

Following their trip to the theatre, the next day saw the team head to Heathrow for the long journey. Nowadays this trip is normally achieved in one overnight eleven hour flight without any refuelling point but in 1962 the route was much more circuitous with a number of stops for fuel. Following the exact route the 1955 Lions team took on what had been the first Lions tour to use air travel, the first stop was Rome where some of the team made their first acquaintance with spaghetti. This was followed by a stop in Khartoum, deep in the African continent where first-time travellers were amazed by the wide expanse of desert surrounding the city. Another stop took place in Nairobi before the Lions eventually landed in Salisbury, the capital of Rhodesia as Zimbabwe was called in those days. The twenty hour flight was an exhausting experience but it was much quicker than the two week leisurely steam boat trip taken by the first Lions tour to South Africa in 1924.

Dave Rollo's own fitness, initially honed on his farm back in Fife along with the training at both Eastbourne and then in Salisbury, combined with his reputation as a sturdy 'never say die' front row player put him in the frame for the first tour match against Rhodesia.

This game was seen as a warm-up for the much tougher matches that would lie ahead when the Lions entered Springbok territory.

However, the home team who ran onto the Hartfield pitch in front of an 11,000 crowd had their tails up having the previous week beaten a British Combined Services team. As the teams lined up for the pre-match formalities, the entertainment was provided by the band of the Rhodesian Rifles playing, among other popular favourites, Colonel Bogey.

Reports of the match recorded that the Lions' "rock solid scrum" with Dave in his favourite tight head position in the front row provided their backs with such a good service they were able to cross the Rhodesian line no fewer than seven times, to which were added a couple of conversions and three penalties to the three penalties for the home side. This gave a final score of thirty eight points to the Lions with nine being gained by the Rhodesian national side.

Fittingly the first try was scored within five minutes by the Lions captain, Arthur Smith, who, playing on the wing, was first on the scene to collect and touch down a punt forward.

Smith had faced strong competition for the honoured position as leader. Others who might have considered they were in line for the captaincy included a number of players who also had previous Lions touring experience; Welshman Bryn Meredith, Irishmen Syd Miller and Bill Mulcahy and Smith's own Scottish colleague, Gordon Waddell.

In those days, the role of captaining a Lions team carried much more responsibility than it does nowadays where specialist forward and back coaches accompany the players on tour. It may seem unbelievable in today's much more structured management that the captain in those days was also largely responsible for organising many of the regular training routines.

The complete management team for that Lions tour consisted of two people plus a liaison officer provided by the South African Rugby Board.

The tour manager was Commander Brian Vaughan who was a former English international. He also served his country as a Naval Commander. Having a military background, he was reckoned to be an excellent disciplinarian. In one of the coincidences that pop up in the most unexpected places, it turned out that Vaughan's brother farmed down in Wales and Dave Rollo had met him before. It turned out they both had a common interest in breeding pedigree Hereford cattle.

Vaughan's assistant was Harry McGibbon, an Irish solicitor who had also played for his country just after the Second World War. Officially he was the under manager and as such he had many of the travel and accommodation issues to sort out.

The third and final member of the management team was a South African who was the main link between the touring party and the hosts. With no medical specialists of their own, the Lions relied on him to contact a local doctor or physiotherapist to sort out all their ailments and injuries. As the tour progressed, this proved to be a vitally important role and it also turned out to be a weak link in the management.

The comparison with today's touring rugby teams, where the players are backed up by highly skilled and specially trained medical staff as well as dieticians and press and communication experts, is hard to avoid.

Injuries were dealt with by the local doctor. Physiotherapy provision was in its infancy. The importance of good food was recognised but little was done specifically to cater for young men burning up loads of calories and as far as press or media work was concerned – it was up to the manager.

The lack of having an "in house" doctor was emphasised within little more than one hour of competitive rugby played in the Lions' first match. One of the Lions was already off the pitch receiving running repairs when another, hooker Stanley Hodgson, had his leg broken. The broken limb was strapped up. A report on the match then records he "returned to the playing field but did not play an active part." This was Hodgson's one and only Lions match on this tour but he was a fitness fanatic. Back in his Co Durham base he went on to play competitive rugby until he was sixty years old. His non-playing contribution to the tour was considered to be so valuable that, rather than send him home as the management did with other injured players, he was asked to stay for the remainder of the trip.

The first game not only introduced the players to the very, very hard ground conditions but also to the constant problem of skin burns resulting from skidding or scraping across the tough unyielding grass. Dave and the other farmer tourists, who included Englishman, Dickie Jeeps, a fruit farmer, reckoned the grass resembled couch – a pernicious weed hated by most farmers. The best way for curing grass burns was, according to the tourists, spraying iodine on the affected area. As Dave recalled after personally experiencing the treatment, "You just got used to it."

The Rhodesian warm-up match over, the team flew down to South Africa where the first match was against Griqualand West based in Kimberley in the Northern Cape. The Lions shuffled their pack and Dave did not feature in the line-up as the management wanted to give all the players who had not taken part in the Rhodesian opener a competitive game. The wholesale changes were none too successful as the South African team held the Lions to an eight all draw.

It was when they were at Kimberley that the Lions took in a tour of the world famous diamond mine where the players were plummeted 6,000 to 7,000 feet into the bowels of the earth in the miners' cage. Down there they could see diamonds being flushed out of the rock by powerful water guns. Apart from a couple of Welsh players who had been coal miners, none of the touring team had been underground so this was a new experience. Dave recalled the intense heat brought about through working closer to the earth's core. He soon realised why they had all been made to strip down to their underpants before donning boiler suits for their underground trip to see the process of extracting the valuable minerals.

Back on the surface, he saw for himself the importance and scale of the diamond industry. The landscape around the mines was man made with huge mountains of spoil having been dumped by the mining companies over previous decades.

The next Lions match was against Western Transvaal in the University town of Potchefstroom where the previous Lions team had come a cropper in 1955. Dave was back in the Lions team at tight head prop and he was playing against an up and coming Springbok who had already been awarded junior national caps. The Transvaal team, which has now changed its name to the Leopards, relied on their powerful pack but the Lions eight held their own and twice crossed their opponents' line, finishing with an eleven points to six advantage. Dave was reckoned by the reporters covering the match to "have gained the better of the front row battle."

Between matches players were expected to help the management team. One of the tasks saw them given a work rota, part of which involved ensuring their team mates were all present, correct and on time; whether it was for breakfast or for being ready for the team bus.

This was not always straightforward as some team members liked a long lie-in and would not get up until the last minute while others would go out for a walk and be late in returning. According to Dave, who took his turn as "duty boy", you had to go up to the bedrooms and shake some of them out of their slumbers while others had to be tracked down to find out where they had gone. "If there was someone missing, the bus wasn't allowed to leave. You had to go back into the hotel and find them. If they were still in their bed they were fined for that."

The team also had a signing session once per week. This involved the entire team sitting around a table signing, then passing on dozens of sheets of paper. The joke among the team members was that it was better to have a short name like Dave Rollo than the much longer one of Mike Campbell-Lamerton. These signed sheets were then handed out at the end of matches to the touchline officials and local dignitaries as mementos of their role in the Lions tour.

Dave did not play in the next two games as the management shuffled their scarce playing resources to suit the varying conditions. In the Cape area both games against Southern Universities and Boland were won by the visitors.

He returned at loose head against South West Africa at Windhoek where he helped the Lions triumph by fourteen points to six. This was another game played at high altitude – 5,600 feet, more than 1,500 feet higher than Ben Nevis – the highest peak in the UK – and a number of visiting players were gasping for breath in the thin air.

This game ended Dave's ambition to play in the Test team against the Springboks. In the opening games he had established himself as the number one tight head prop in the Lions group but late in the South West Africa match he pulled a floating muscle in the ribcage in his back. Nowadays, that would have entailed a visit to the hospital to be x-rayed and after proper treatment he could have resumed playing. In the 1962 Lions tour there were neither doctors nor medical backup. He was just strapped up and he lost weeks when, with proper treatment, he could have been playing.

In his absence, Kingsley Jones came in to play in the tight head slot and the Welshman then held the position for all four of the Test matches, the first of which Dave watched with his ribcage all bandaged up. Despite losing out to him, Dave and Kingsley, whose father was a fruit and vegetable trader back in Wales, formed a friendship that endured beyond the Lions trip.

One of the features of this lengthy Lions tour, which included staying in more than twenty different hotels, was a policy of constantly changing the players sharing the twin bedrooms. This successfully prevented cliques being created.

It was during the Lions' visit to South West Africa – now Namibia – that Dave discovered the cattle and sheep in that country were suffering from foot and mouth disease. Outbreaks had been occurring for more than seven years. Having seen a funeral pyre of foot and mouth disease infected cattle on his neighbouring farm in Fife in the 1950s, he was amazed the local farmers were doing nothing about the virulent and highly infectious disease. "They just let the animals that had it die and the ones that weren't affected survived."

In the match against Northern Transvaal prior to the first Test, the *Times* reporter described the play as being more suited to a Roman arena than to a sports pitch. Of particular note was the right hook delivered by Mannetjies Roux, playing for the 'Boks. This smashed the cheekbone of the Lions' star stand-off Richard Sharp and took him out of contention for the next few weeks. Curiously or coincidentally an identical injury had been inflicted on the star Lions player in a previous tour in the game against the same opposition. After the match, Lions tour manager Brian Vaughan called for a ban on high tackles; an issue which is still contentious to the present day.

The Lions lost the game fourteen points to six and only subsequently managed a three points all draw in the second Test with more than half a dozen of their players, including Sharp and Rollo, on the injured list.

Back on rugby duty, after being certified as being fit enough to play, Dave came into action against Natal where again the Lions pack were credited with giving their three-quarters players sufficient good ball to ensure a thirteen points to three victory. He was credited by the opposing front row as helping Lions hooker Herbert Goodwin win the front row battle by nine tight heads to four; these being the days where hooking the ball as it came into the scrum was considered a skill as opposed to the present day front row battle based largely on sheer avoirdupois.

Despite winning the Natal match, there were no easy matches for the touring team and playing two games per week against strong opposition took its toll on the Lions' limited resources. Even after years of international opposition both in the Five Nations and against top touring parties of Wallabies and All Blacks, Dave reckoned the props he met on the South African tour had the hardest muscle.

He believed this was down to the amount of meat the 'Boks ate. On the Lions bus travelling from match to match or even just out sightseeing, he was amazed at the number of farm shops at the side of the roads. Nowadays this is a regular sight in the UK but back in the sixties it was hardly known. One of the main sales in the South African shops was meat. This was mainly beef and it was advertised as such but Dave was intrigued by the appearance of monkey gland steak and decided to try it. Before doing so, he found out the meat being used in the steak was beef and not from a tree swinging primate. The name of this popular South African dish is based on the sauce or dressing which includes a strong mixture of garlic, onions and ketchup. Preferring straightforward steak, Dave decided this was not an experience he would repeat.

Only four days after the Natal game, Dave pulled on the Lions jersey once again. This time the opposition was Eastern Province who, in their Port Elizabeth base, had dented the winning streak of a previous Lions team. They had a reputation for toughness and the match report recorded, "This was a robust match, especially up front, but there were no chinks in the winners' armour." The score was decisively twenty one points to three for the Lions.

Dave (first left) playing against the Junior Springboks at Pretoria.

He was not picked for the game against the Orange Free State which was drawn fourteen points all but was back in action for the match against the Junior Springboks at Pretoria which ended up with a sixteen points to eleven victory after a late second half surge by the Lions. This match was also marked by further damage to the Rollo nose as it was broken during the game, thus replicating an injury he suffered in his first ever international game against England. The injury cannot have detracted from his playing performance as he was recorded as playing his part in the late Lions push to victory.

While at Pretoria, the Lions visited one of the gold mines in the area. There was a popular rumour at this mine that whoever could lift a bar of pure gold with one hand could keep it. This myth was based on the sheer weight of the precious metal and the fact that it would be too heavy for a single hand to lift. Dave said that the players were aware of the rumour and were up for the challenge but unfortunately were not allowed to go near the gold as it was heavily protected.

There was a sequel to their visit, as the Lions tour bus was delayed on its departure from the mine. Gordon Waddell had mischievously entered under "purpose of visit" the single word "theft". The mine owners did not share his sense of humour and he was thoroughly searched before being allowed out. Waddell, who was the son of one of Scotland's most famous rugby players, Herbert Waddell, was later to live in South Africa where he married the daughter of a mining magnate and became a director of several mining companies. Later in life, he was elected to the South African Parliament as a member of the Progressive Party.

From Pretoria, it was a short distance to the Lions' next port of call – the university town of Potchefstroom – where they would play the roughest, toughest match of the tour against a Combined Services team.

The Lions won twenty points to six but, reflecting on the game afterwards, even the South African team manager described it as, "sheer thuggery". Still recovering from the nose broken in the Junior Springboks match, Dave missed that game and the following one against the Western Provinces played in Cape Town, which the Lions won by twenty one points to thirteen.

The constant criss-crossing of South Africa was a feature of the tour with the majority of the miles being covered by the team coach which Dave said was always surrounded by curious locals whenever it stopped.

South Africa was still a strictly segregated country in those days and none of the games the Lions played were against sides with black or coloured players.

Segregation was very noticeable wherever the Lions went. The stadia where the games were played were divided and even the toilets were segregated. "Within the segregated grounds, I reckoned the Lions' biggest supporters were the black South Africans because they wanted to see the white South Africans being beaten."

Apart from their visit to the theatre in London before they left where they saw a satirical take on segregated life in South Africa, the Lions were given no special briefing on the question of colour or race before their departure from London. The attitude of the management seemed to be that such matters did not involve those playing rugby.

Dave recalled, "We were never told not to mix with the black people. It was mostly coloured people working in the hotels and they were great. At our hotel they couldn't do enough to help you. As with any white touring team that was visiting they wanted them to beat the Springboks.

"They all knew about us. They must have read up about us. For example, they knew I had come from Cupar and played for the Howe of Fife so they were pretty well up to date with their sports."

Thirty five years later, Dave and another Scottish cap, Ron Glasgow visited South Africa with the 1997 British Lions team. The country had abandoned its apartheid policy and Dave was amazed at the transformation with segregation now consigned to the dustbin of history.

Fully recovered from his nose break, Dave was listed in the pack that dominated South Western Districts in Oudshoorn which the Lions won eleven points to three. Oudshoorn is ostrich farming country and here the pre-match diversion included a visit to an ostrich farm. Anybody who fancied a ride on an ostrich could have a go but the Lions soon found out they were no match for the birds. Dave reckoned, "If you could last for five seconds you were lucky."

His on-field performances put him on the bench for the second Test where a pre-match report recorded that he and his colleagues "inspired full confidence." This match in Durban will forever be remembered as the one where the referee was the only person in the 30,000 crowd or the thirty on-field players who did not see the Lions score the try that would have levelled the final score. Pushing the ball over the try line the whole Lions pack collapsed on top of it. The hapless official claimed he could not identify the scorer. "I just lost sight of the ball," he admitted later.

Although he did not play in that game, Dave was involved in the next against Northern Universities where the Lions came away with what was reported as a "lucky draw." The Lions backs were blamed for an inept performance while the pack was excused.

One of the big non Test matches followed in Johannesburg when the Lions played Transvaal. Under the eyes off 50,000 spectators, including those of the Prime Minister Dr Hendrik Verwoerd who was credited with being the "father of apartheid" and who was assassinated four years later, the Lions steamrollered the opposition 24-3.

Transvaal had four Springboks in their side but the Lions forwards were reckoned to have "played a fine game with hooker Meredith having the advantage, thanks to his strong props, Syd Miller and Dave Rollo." The game was notable with Sharp coming back from his broken cheekbone injury to score fifteen of the winning points total.

Sharp was included in the third Test match to be held in Cape Town but Dave once again had to occupy what has been called the worst seat in the stadium; the substitutes' bench. The Lions lost the match by eight points to three.

He was however back in the team which demolished North Western Districts by thirty four points to eight in Burgersdorp; a town with a population similar to Cupar and thus one of the smallest in which the Lions played.

With twenty matches played and more than two months since they had left Great Britain, the travelling Lions were showing signs of weariness. For some of the Welsh players a visit to the liner the *Transvaal Castle* in the harbour at Cape Town was a bad idea as it spawned a whole bout of homesickness after they met some of the many Welsh workers on the boat. The boat had a Scottish connection having been built in John Brown's shipyard in Glasgow two years previously specifically for the journey between the UK and South Africa.

Throughout the tour communications were far removed from today's world where contact can easily be made across the globe. For the 1960s Lions it was a case of writing letters. In Dave's case, he had written letters to Jean wondering how she and daughter Pat were getting on. His mother, Nan also wanted to know what life in South Africa was like. He wrote once a week to both but this writing effort was easily eclipsed by Richard Sharp whose girlfriend received a letter detailing every single day's work and play.

Now with the end of the tour in sight the tourists travelled to East London where they dispatched Border by the slim margin of five points to nil. Dave did not play in that match but midweek he played in the team that beat Central Universities at Port Elizabeth fourteen points to six. This was one of a number of occasions when the Scots in the team were encouraged by the skirl of the pipes as the teams were piped onto the field by the Port Elizabeth Caledonian Pipe Band.

Off the field, the six Scots, along with two press-ganged team members from Wales, often put on a dancing display with a version of an Eightsome reel. One observer to this dancing display, commentator Vivian Jenkins, noted "Rollo is surprisingly light on his feet for such a hefty individual." Jenkins did not know Dave had, from an early age, been encouraged to learn Scottish country dancing by his mother.

Dave and a few other traditionally dressed Scots also attempted to

A kilted Dave tries out an African rickshaw in Durban.

learn some of the native dancing that had been provided by Zulus, thus they earned the nickname of the "kilted warriors".

Their dancing prowess was no use in the next game at Springs where the Eastern Transvaal team had the better of the Lions who were trying to rest some of their better players for the final Test match the following week.

Before the fourth and final Test match the tour party took in the world famous Kruger National Park where the travelling Lions saw real lions as well as a whole range of other wild animals. It was here that Dave gained the nickname of being "The Prince" with Gordon Waddell describing him as such in a post-dinner speech. As happens all across the world, where links are made through those who have long ago left their native country, it was here that Dave met up with friends of his wife who had emigrated from their home in Dollar to manage a large fruit farm.

Earlier, in similar fashion in Cape Town he had bumped into a friend of the owner of the cafe in Cupar where schoolboy Dave would buy a hot orange drink during school lunch hour.

The break in Kruger did not help build the Lions' confidence as the fourth Test saw them demolished by thirty four points to fourteen in an open running game. After a keenly contested first hour of the match, the home side ran over the visibly tiring visitors in the final twenty minutes. The Scottish skipper Arthur Smith did not play, claiming injury but there was a view that he wanted fellow Scot, Ronnie Cowan to gain a Test match cap. Subsequently Cowan signed professional forms to play rugby league immediately he stepped off the plane back in the UK. The move by Smith rubbed salt in Dave's wound as his chance to play a Lions Test match had slipped by through being unnecessarily side-lined through a badly treated injury.

The post mortem on the 1962 Lions trip concluded that the itinerary was too demanding and it was therefore to be the last tour of that length. It had also, from the first game, been bedevilled by injuries with the medical back-up poor to non-existent. In assessing the players, it was reckoned the forwards were the only department to inspire confidence and there was a special positive mention of the front row mafia.

The fourth Test match was the final game in South Africa but the Lions had one more game to play on their flight home. In Nairobi they played against East Africa. The difference in quality between the two sides saw the Lions coast home by fifty points to zero. After two months playing without a drop of rain falling, the tourists were returning to the wetter climate of Great Britain so when the visit to Kenya brought with it rain it was a wonderful acclimatisation.

Dave played in the East Africa match thus completing thirteen games wearing the famous Lions strip but where had this journey to the top of the rugby playing world begun?

CHAPTER TWO

EARLY YEARS

FARMING IN THE 1930s was not profitable. Prices for grain, cattle and sheep had soared in the World War One years and for a short spell afterwards. Then, when normal trade resumed and imported food arrived from countries all around the world, the prices farmers received for their grain, potatoes, beef and lamb fell dramatically. Farmers survived by either being good at their job or good at tightening their belts.

John Rollo who farmed at Wester Forret five miles on the north side of Cupar was proficient in both of these. He had taken the tenancy of the 426 acre mixed livestock and arable farm in 1901 as a twenty five year old and had been through both good and bad times. His father had been a miller at the small farm of Forret Mill which was on the same estate as Wester Forret. It meant that John's whole life was centred in one square mile in North Fife.

The cash crops John grew included barley which was and remains a vital ingredient in making Scotland's iconic drink, whisky. Another cereal crop which was a mainstay in the rotation was oats; a crop which noted wordsmith, Samuel Johnston somewhat cynically defined as good for feeding horses in England but used to feed men in Scotland. Rye was also grown on Wester Forret in the early days of the last century but demand for the crop to make bread slipped away with wheat being preferred by the millers. Potatoes were also grown on the fertile soil and, in winter, railway van loads were sent by train from the local Kilmany railway station to help feed those living in the big cities of Edinburgh

Dave overlooking the family farm of Wester Forret from Forret Hill.

and Glasgow. One crop, which is hardly ever seen today but which was important as animal feed in bygone days, was a mixture of peas and beans. The protein-rich end product was called mashlam and was used to fatten sheep as well as feed the workhorses on the farm.

In the days before tractors came on the scene it was reckoned that a pair of workhorses was needed for every 100 acres of crop so John Rollo had three pair, plus an odd one.

As many farmers did in those days John married late in life. He was fifty years old when he met Agnes Durie who was some thirty years younger. Nan, as she was always known, came from farming stock as her family farmed Newcairnie little more than a couple of miles to the west of Forret.

Their first born son Ian came into the world in 1924 to be followed ten years later with the arrival on 7th July 1934 of David Miller Durie Rollo; Dave's middle names coming respectively from a relative in Edinburgh and his mother's maiden name.

Both boys were born at home and, as was the case in those days, their playground was the farm and in particular the buildings that made up the farm steading.

Along with the sons and daughters of the farm workers Dave and his older brother would play in the stables that housed the horses, in the granary where the feed for the cattle and sheep was kept and in the turnip shed or feed store for the cattle in winter. Another part of their playground was the cattle courts where the bullocks were fattened prior to heading to the local market in Cupar.

With all their nooks and crannies, these old stone-built buildings with pantiled roofs were ideal for playing traditional games like hide and seek, while the cobbled yard outside the stables was an ideal base for playing other popular games of those days such as kick the can.

The Rollo family on Ian's wedding day with Ian (left) and Dave (right) flanking father and mother, John and Nan.

Primary schooling for Dave and the farmworkers' children living in the farm cottages at Wester Forret involved a two mile walk along a farm track to the hamlet of Logie where the single teacher parish school was situated close to the parish church.

Miss Stewart, as she was called by all the 30 or so pupils, was responsible for their early education and she was determined that her charges would be as proficient as they could be in the three Rs; Reading, wRiting and aRithmetic that used to be considered the core of a child's education. Of these three, she was a stickler for good writing as she saw it as a way for all youngsters, regardless of their academic ability, to advance in the world. From his first days in Primary one through to his final year in Primary seven, Dave was taught to write legibly and neatly, although he admits that other subjects such as singing were totally omitted from his education; something his rugby team mates later in life found out.

Along with Jack Black, the son of a neighbouring farmer, he would make the two mile trip in the morning and back every afternoon for the seven years from 1939 to the summer of 1945. There were no concessions or days off on account of bad weather, although a snowy winter could bring added excitement as it often involved a little sledging and snowballing on the daily trip. On spring and summer days with no darkness urging the boys home, they would often make a slight diversion off the track to school when they went to play around the Forret curling pond. In the height of a dry summer, the water in the pond would evaporate and the boys were able to get to the blue clay lining of the pond. A handful of the clay would be taken home where it would be rolled into small balls and placed in the oven. After drying out, Dave would have his own self-made marbles to take to school the next day.

In cold winters this pond would freeze over and the local farmers and other worthies would meet in an afternoon to have a game of curling. Dave's father was a keen, keen curler and in due course this enthusiasm was passed down to both Ian and Dave although Dave admits other sports, especially rugby, soon took priority.

Another ploy for the small boys walking to and from school was to try and emulate their parents by smoking. Not having tobacco to hand, they made do with using the hollow stalks of cow parsley plants filled with the seeds of docken plants. Thankfully the mix was neither poisonous nor hallucinogenic and the boys survived their apprenticeship in smoking. In later life, apart from the odd cigar, Dave, unlike some of his rugby playing colleagues who smoked cigarettes, never succumbed to the habit.

Sometimes, when he was slightly older but still at primary school, Dave's mother and father allowed him to take his Shetland pony, called Punch, to save him walking all the way to school. When this happened, the pony was left in the glebe which was the land given to the parish minister to keep the horse he needed for his pastoral duties.

On those days when school was over Dave would saddle up and make the return trip. But on one occasion, Punch decided to roll over on the newly cut stubble, leaving its rider to make a hasty jump out of the saddle to prevent being crushed and then an equally swift jump back into the saddle as the pony got back on to its feet.

Dave's primary schoolboy days coincided with the country being at war but little of this impacted on him, although when the whins on the hill behind the quarry at Wester Forret were set alight one night, there was a panic. It was thought the fire had been started deliberately by enemy agents to guide aeroplanes to target nearby Leuchars airfield. Firemen from all the local stations were summoned but it took the best part of a week to extinguish the blaze.

As was also common in those war torn days, local houses were used to billet servicemen from abroad. In the case of the Rollo family, they hosted two Canadian Air Force officers. This was the first time Dave had come into contact with the military and their uniforms but while he remembers little of the men themselves, he does recall they once left bars of chocolate. Chocolate was prized when food rationing was in force and Dave had never seen anything like it. His mother hid the bars in a cupboard in the parlour and it was only given out in small portions when Dave and his brother had behaved themselves. This was a good rationing system until one day the drawer was opened and, not unusually for farmhouses in those days, it came as a bitter disappointment to find that a small rodent had feasted on the chocolate.

The servicemen left early in June 1944 just before D-Day when the Allied armies crossed the Channel and fought the Germans on mainland Europe. Such was the transient nature of war Dave never saw either of them again.

He did however see other servicemen at Wester Forret but for the Italian prisoners working in the fields at the grain harvest and picking potatoes their war was over and they seemed much happier being in the fields rather than in battle. They were stationed at the nearby camp of Annfield near Ladybank and were transported in old army trucks. The prisoners must not have been seen as a threat and came without guards.

Perhaps, they saw Ian – Dave's brother – heading off to the hall in the nearby village of Luthrie where twice a week all the volunteers in the Home Guard would carry out their drills practising for an invasion that never occurred. They only had imitation wooden rifles with which to practise their military moves but they were introduced to other weapons of war like hand grenades. The enthusiastic amateurs were taught how to remove the pin to activate the grenade and then to lob it at the target. Dave was told some of the older farmhands were good at one of those operations but coordinating it with the second caused the instructors a few anxious moments.

After seven years at Logie school, the next stage in life saw Dave head into Cupar to Bell Baxter secondary school. For most pupils living in country areas, this was a case of getting to some point on the school bus circuit. For Dave this involved a one mile bike ride to the Denbrae road end where the school bus collected a group of children for the remaining five mile trip to Cupar. To call the twelve-seater Ford shooting brake a bus was an exaggeration but after a year or so, with more pupils to be taken to school, it was replaced by a proper bus. This time it was a vehicle with wooden seats which were a source of great fun and nonsense as the youngsters deliberately slipped to and fro as the vehicle swung around the twisty rural roads.

Getting to school for Dave and his pals was relatively straightforward until the Great Storm of 1947 occurred. After a mild start to the winter, February was the coldest on record and it coincided with a massive snow storm which blocked roads throughout Scotland. Men cut through the snow drifts but the roads were then blocked up for a second time. Five weeks passed before Dave and the other children from the surrounding farms were able to resume their schooling; not that they were too concerned about that especially as there were lots of ploys that they could, and did get up to on the farm.

There were also ploys in Cupar for Dave and his pals and one night Dave, aged a mere twelve years old, borrowed the family car without his parents' permission. Dave drove it safely to Cupar and back but that did not mean he avoided his father's wrath on his return to the farm.

Soon after that episode, Dave, after seeing a Tarzan film, decided he wanted to build a tree house in one of the chestnut trees that overlooked both the farm and the steading; a place where he could see all that was going on from his lofty perch. It is testimony to his skills that the small six foot by four foot house in the tree survived not only his childhood but that of his daughter. When Dave came out of the farm in 1985 the shed was still in place and when this was pointed out to the auctioneer conducting the farm sale, it was quickly 'knocked down' to the incoming farmer for £10 – not a bad price for a fifty year old hut.

His woodworking skills may have been honed at Bell Baxter where technical subjects were taught by Mr Wilson, known informally by all his pupils as Weary Willie. Dave would testify that his teaching was far from being tedious. If Mr Wilson considered the class was not paying sufficient attention, after going quietly to the back of the classroom, he would throw the duster at the blackboard; thus immediately snapping any slumbering pupils out of their dreams.

Although coming from a small rural school into a secondary with hundreds of pupils was quite a cultural shock for Dave, it was tempered a little by knowing his class teacher, Mrs Sinclair, as she was the wife of his local parish minister.

He also met up with fellow pupil Willie Bell whose parents, once a week, played cards with Dave's mother and father. Willie was a year ahead of Dave and he knew his way about the school and also, importantly, the places you could get food down in the town of Cupar in preference to the school lunches. First stop on the dinner time trip down town was to the Co-operative where a sausage roll could be bought from its baker's shop. This kept the pangs of hunger away from Dave and Willie until they reached the Temperance Hotel where their preferred diet was either soup followed by rissoles or rissoles followed by custard pudding. Either way the cost of lunch was nine old pence or four pence in today's money.

If there was any spare pocket money, or if he was still feeling hungry, another stop on the way back to school was the small sweet shop owned by Mr McDonald adjacent to the La Scala cinema. There for two old pennies, a Lyons ice cream could be bought; it was one of Dave's favourites.

One afternoon a week saw his class marched up to the Duffus Park where they played football on the Cupar Hearts pitch. In those days, it was just a field and the local farmer was allowed to graze his sheep, which meant players had to watch what they stepped into or where they fell.

In a system which operated at that time at Bell Baxter, boys in the more academic streams at school were encouraged to play rugby while football was the order of the day for the rest.

In those days Dave preferred football having played informal versions of the game from an early age. Later in life he claimed the ball control skills he picked up at school helped him when he made it on the international rugby scene whenever the ball was bobbling along the ground.

His PE teacher, Jock Blair was one of the many members of staff who had come back from military service and his gym classes were designed to challenge the boys. He was a strict disciplinarian but Dave, unlike other boys and especially his old school pal Jack, never felt the 'Lochgelly' which is what the leather strap used to instil discipline was called.

Unsurprisingly for someone who had been brought up on a farm and was used to hard work, even as a boy, Dave did well at the annual school sports. Although he did not fare as well as his brother Ian who had been junior school sports champion.

Dave excelled at sprint events, the high jump and the shot put but these performances were only sufficient to get him into the runner-up spot in the overall championship.

Dave left school aged fifteen. His mother was ill at that time – although she rallied and lived for another forty years – and his father wanted him to stay at home so he didn't sit any exams before he left Bell Baxter. From an early age he knew he wanted to farm so his father's wish suited him down to the ground.

His first working day saw him, a fifteen year old boy, ploughing with a pair of Clydesdale horses. The job he turned out was judged as quite satisfactory but the lure of more horsepower saw him move onto tractor work.

The farm had bought its first tractor, a Case, in the mid 1930s and in the early days of the Second World War, because of an urgency to produce more food from farms within the UK, a second in the shape of a Fordson was then bought. This became Dave's tractor. In line with what was happening all over the country, gradually mechanical horsepower took over from traditional horsepower and before the end of the 1950s all the workhorses at Wester Forret had gone.

Like all young people starting off in work, Dave remembers his first pay. In his case it was the princely sum of one pound which a year later in 1951 was doubled. In early 1954 Dave was called through to Edinburgh for a medical prior to heading off to serve two years' National Service – still compulsory in the post-war years. Although he had been keen to

Dave on his favourite tractor getting
ready for a ploughing match.

work on the farm, the chance to see the wider world appealed and he
put his name down for the Navy. He did this despite the fact that young
men joining the Senior Service were required to spend more than two
years in uniform unlike those serving in the Army and Air Force where
conscripts could leave after twenty four months.

All of this became irrelevant as at the beginning of August his father
died and Dave was exempted from carrying out any National Service.
He and his brother went into partnership to run the farm.

CHAPTER THREE

A LATE START TO RUGBY

FOR A PLAYER who ended up playing forty times for his country and who also played for the British Lions, his was not a particularly auspicious start. Dave had been picked for the Howe of Fife second fifteen against Perthshire Rugby Club's equivalent.

This was his first ever game of rugby. He had alongside him in the front row of the scrum his old school pal, Willie Bell. In the world of the front row mafia, Willie had assured Dave he would keep him right and sure enough he did just that. In a loose ruck, Dave had seen the ball at his feet and having speedily picked it up and tucked it under his arm, headed off towards the try line. A loud shout from Willie stopped him in his tracks. "Dave. You're going the wrong way."

He was nineteen years old when he first picked up the oval ball. After leaving school and working on the family farm, his main sporting activity had been playing football. The games he played were not rigidly organised. His team did not belong to a league. It was just a collection of farm workers getting together twice a week to have a kick about. "First to arrive would be captain of one side, and the second would be captain of the other side," he recalls. "It could be twenty-a-side."

When the team which did not have a name travelled to away games, they were transported in the back of a farm trailer provided by Met Graham, who farmed next door to the Rollos at Kedlock. The tractor and trailer transport took the informal team to neighbouring parishes such as Luthrie and Gauldry where they played similarly ad hoc local teams. Sometimes, in response to a challenge from further afield, they ventured to Leuchars or Strathkinnes.

The matches they contested with other make-shift teams provided neither points nor silverware. The main reward was the bragging rights that victory brought. None of the teams had a set strip. A few of the players had football boots but many of the ploughmen played in their everyday tackety boots; thus ensuring some robust tackles. As many of the pitches on which they played also had an everyday use as fields for grazing cattle, there was the additional hazard of taking a tumble into a cowpat.

The playing season was from May to the beginning of August. This was not because, unlike professional players, they preferred playing in the summer. That period in the year after the rush of spring work and before the busy harvest period, was a quiet time on the farms. Generally there was no overtime work on the farm and the workers' evenings were free.

The informal playing season also suited as the games and the travel to and fro were all carried out in the long summer daylight hours. Games were played for no set length of time with the lowering of the sun towards the horizon being the rough timekeeper. With neither head nor tail lights on their transporting tractors and trailers, the teams often returned home in the gathering dusk.

And that was Dave's sporting life until his school pal, Willie Bell, urged Dave and his father to come along and watch a rugby match. It was not love at first sight. The rules seemed complex to a casual onlooker.

It would be another year before Dave was persuaded to join the Howe of Fife; a club he remains a member of more than sixty years later.

The Howe of Fife club he joined was in one way relatively young and in another could stretch back into the previous century. It had come into existence in May 1946 through the amalgamation of Cupar Rugby Club, whose existence could be traced back to 1874, and a previous Howe of Fife club based in Ladybank which was formed in 1921.

The Cupar club, with its lengthier history, had played in a number of sites in and around Cupar in its earlier days including the Cart Haugh. This location used to be the base for the showground of the North Fife Foal Show in the years of horsepower as well as being the site for the predecessor of the Fife Agricultural Show.

The old Howe based in the railway town of Ladybank, stressed its rural roots by renting its playing pitch – a grass field – from a neighbouring farmer for a figure which could vary depending on the price of potatoes in any particular year. The Ladybank location was no accident as rail transport was often the preferred method of travelling for teams in the early years of the last century and Ladybank was on the main north/south line.

The 'new' Howe originally played at Wetlands which had been acquired by Fife Council. Its sloping playing fields were used through the week by Bell Baxter School. By the time Dave joined the Howe in 1953, it had moved its playing base to the Duffus Park. This park, gifted to the townspeople, continues to the present day to provide the club with its pitches.

The training regime for the Howe players in the 1950s was straightforward. Every Monday night during the season, they met in the gym at Bell Baxter School. This was where a few years earlier Dave and many of his colleagues in the Howe had had their PE or physical education classes when they were at school. The similarity was magnified for many of them as the coach putting the players through their paces was their old school teacher Jock Blair.

The assumption was that those turning up for training were already physically fit. Many of the Howe players worked on farms and this involved a great deal of hard graft. On his farm, Dave handled hundredweight bags of potatoes. In modern terms these would be fifty kilos and when the bags were filled they would be manhandled onto trailers. Other farm work that involved considerable physical effort and consequential muscle building included clearing stones off fields where crops were to be grown and handling cattle and sheep. The ability to deal with livestock weighing anything between a few kilos and a tonne is a skill that occasionally needs a bit of muscle power.

Some special Scottish training – Dave lifting 20 kilo curling stones above his head.

As if this exercise was not sufficient to prove someone's fitness, when it came to morning and afternoon breaks on farms, the workers would often challenge each other to feats of strength. One favourite challenge would be to pick up the two twenty-five kilo weights (or 56 pounds). These were used to weigh the potatoes. The workers would then lift the weights up above their head just as weightlifters do with proper weights. On Dave's Wester Forret farm there was another form of challenge. This involved one of the workers lying face down on the ground and a sack filled with fifty kilos of grain was laid across his back. From that prone position, the challenge was to stand upright with the sack still on your back.

All of the regular farm tasks and all of the nonsense challenges were good for building muscle as Dave found when he suffered a slight injury on the farm one day. When he went to the local GP, Dr Willie Preston, the good doctor declared he had never seen such strong arm muscles.

Despite his body strength, Dave did feel he might be lacking when it came to running about rugby pitches and so he tried to put some miles on his personal clock. One day after finishing work, he set off for the village of Rathillet meaning to take a triangular route before returning back home some six miles later. Two and a bit miles into this run, he decided long distance running was not for him and he took a short cut back home across the fields. This did not however signal the end of his running training as a couple of nights later he went onto the main road just outside the farm and, using the telephone poles as distance markers, measured out 200 yards. Then it was a case of doing loops of that distance out and back. In his own version of interval training, he did eight of those every evening with the final two being done in full sprint mode. This routine, which he carried out throughout his rugby career, was a regular exercise every night except when he went to Cupar for specialist rugby training on a Monday. Sometimes he even carried out this training regime on a Saturday night after a match. He always reckoned that tough schedule gave him all the stamina he needed for the eighty minutes of a game regardless of how tough it was.

With physical fitness assured, the Howe training in Dave's early rugby playing days was very much concentrated on improving ball handling skills. The routine the coach put the players through was very simple. They formed a big circle round the gym with two players in the middle. The outside players ran around with the ball being passed back and forward to the two in the centre. A whistle from Jock Blair saw the players turn round to go the other way so those taking part could learn how to pass the ball off the other foot. The only variation on this routine was changing the pair of players in the middle. The emphasis throughout was on improving ball handling skills; training which stood Dave in good stead throughout his playing career.

Dave in typical fashion fending off the opposition.

Back in the 1950s there were no on-site changing rooms at the Duffus Park and players would troop back and forward or, in the case of the more prosperous, drive the one mile plus between the Park and the Royal Hotel; the latter hostelry providing the Howe with two hotel rooms; one for the home team and the other for the opposition.

After a wet muddy match, the single bath in room seven – the Howe's changing room – often had a fair amount of sludge in it which then had to be scooped out to prevent choking the drains. The hotel management must have reckoned that the income from the bar after the match would easily cover any plumbing costs. The odds of wedding guests at receptions held in the hotel on a Saturday afternoon objecting to rubbing shoulders with two teams of muddied players arriving after a match were still in favour of the bar beer sales.

The Royal also provided a base for post-training night refreshments. For the farmers in the Howe, there was an added bonus in this Monday night socialising as a number of Edinburgh and Glasgow grain and potato merchants used to stay in the hotel on Monday night because the auction market in Cupar was held on a Tuesday.

Being based in the centre of an agricultural area has over the years provided the Howe with a source of physically strong players. It also used to mean that the club had a reputation for being slow starters to the playing season with many of its star players still working at bringing in the harvest in August and September.

This problem meant Dave initially did not get into the first fifteen as he gave priority to getting the harvest in at home. By the time he was free on a Saturday the team was already made up. On his first trip with the first team, he was down as travelling reserve. On arrival at Alloa, the Howe found their opposition was short of a player and they volunteered Dave in order to match up the numbers. His performance that day was not recorded but at the selection meeting for the next game, the Howe captain, Gordon Stewart, declared that the Alloa game would be the last in which Dave played against the Howe. Thereafter he was a fixture in the first fifteen for the next decade and a half and every Monday morning in the playing season he received the all-important postcard indicating both his selection and the team departure time from the Royal Hotel.

His preferred position was as tight head in the front row of the scrum but he could also play on the loose head side. This flexibility was used by the selectors of the Howe and later by the Scottish and British Lions team managers as it gave them options.

It also gave Dave a claim to have had played with four different numbers on his back because in the pre-1960s, the front row of the scrum were numbered 10, 9 and 8. Then in a reversal of numbering throughout the rugby world, the front row picked up the numbers 1, 2 and 3.

In actuality, Dave once played with another number on his back after one of the selectors decided this strong running farmer should be given a chance to show his skills as well and provide a bit more strength in the centre of the three-quarter line. He had never played in that position before and afterwards this tough front row player declared he had never played in such a tough encounter as he nursed bruises from the number of knocks he had taken. "People came and hit me when I was carrying the ball. I will never play in that position again," he declared.

The games the Howe played in those days were almost universally against others in the Midlands District and this saw them not only take on other Fife teams, such as their nearest and oldest 'enemy' Madras in St Andrews, but also Dunfermline Rugby Club which was flying high in those days. One of the oldest clubs in the area, Kirkcaldy always provided strong opposition as did Perthshire.

It was against these and other teams in the area that Dave picked up his first honour as he was a member of the Howe sevens team that won the Midlands Cup in 1957.

Although the Howe committee had urged their colleagues in the Midlands to form a league so there could be a marker for success, other Midlands clubs were not in favour and the proposal fell. It would not be until the 1973/74 season before league rugby was introduced.

Successful Howe team in the Midlands Sevens 1957. Back row: Dave, Danny Gough, Bob Norman, Bob Steven. Front row: Bert Gibson, Tom Pearson (captain), Willie Bell.

In the meantime, the old informal system of playing purely to gain bragging rights against their neighbours continued. For the Howe, this required either a train journey to play in Dundee against the High School or Harris FP or a ferry boat trip across the Tay in those pre-road bridge days if games outwith Dundee were on the cards.

A game on the north side of the Tay also ensured that post-match hospitality was not extended too long as the last ferry to Fife left Dundee about 10 o' clock. Sometimes, if the post-match socialising was still going on, the Howe would send one of their number to ask the captain of the ferry boat if he could delay the departure. On other occasions, it took a flying leap from the quayside to board the departing boat. Missing the ferry back home to Fife entailed a long road trip round by Perth.

Gradually, as transport became easier, the Howe extended their playing options with trips to Aberdeen and Edinburgh appearing on their schedule. Again, travelling south, if the game was not in Edinburgh itself, it often involved a ferry trip across the Forth with similar time restrictions on the journey home. Sometimes the Howe travelled over to Edinburgh by train but this was fraught with problems. On one occasion, Dave and his pal, Willie Bell, were fast asleep as the train stopped in Kirkcaldy where their car had been left. When they woke up, the carriage had been shunted into a siding in Thornton several miles away. It was late and there were no taxis around so the bold pair had to walk back to Kirkcaldy to get their car. They were not going to make that mistake again so next time the Howe were playing in Edinburgh, they boarded the train in Cupar. Sadly they were again fast asleep as the train went past Cupar. Next stop was Dundee and it was the last train for the night. Thankfully Willie had a farmer friend outside the city who did not mind rescuing the pair and putting them up for the night.

Apart from that occasion, the rule, regardless of the location of the Saturday game or the lateness of the hour when the post-match festivities finished, next morning saw Dave, the farmer, back in his working clothes feeding his hungry sheep and cattle who did not care a jot that it was a Sunday morning. There is no such thing as a day of rest on a livestock farm.

CHAPTER FOUR

FAME, FARMING AND FIANCÉE

EVEN IN THE 70,000 strong crowd the Scottish voices could be heard clearly. One shouted, "Get up on your feet Dave. We have paid a lot of money to see you play for eighty minutes. You are not getting off with just playing twenty." But Dave was not quite ready to get up.

He had been knocked unconscious and was lying on his back on the Twickenham turf with blood pouring out of his broken nose. It was a mere twenty minutes into the 1959 Calcutta Cup match between Scotland and England and it was Dave Rollo's first international cap. He had tackled the English winger from behind and his face, or more specifically his nose, had hit the back of the Englishman's head. The accident had not happened, as local legend would later claim, as a result of some English skulduggery. In those days before substitutes were allowed, the situation was serious both for Dave and for the Scottish team. There he was flat out after only a few minutes and there was his team looking as if it might have to play the remainder of the match one man down. Dave was made of sterner stuff. After regaining consciousness, he went off the field and for the next ten minutes, cotton wool was stuffed up his nose to stop the bleeding.

This proving successful, he returned to the fray seemingly unaffected, with newspaper reports praising him for his role in a game which ended up in a three all draw. He was described as "going harder" than any of the rest of the fifteen forwards on the field. He played his part in a match which most impartial observers reckoned Scotland could have

Dave was knocked unconscious after twenty minutes
in his first international in March 1959 at Twickenham.

won if their twenty two year old stand-off captain, Gordon Waddell, had played more of a running game rather than just punting the ball up into English territory.

In his book *Talking of Rugby*, commentating legend Bill McLaren referred to Dave's courage in coming back onto the pitch where he played with "undiminished fire."

One very biased spectator in the crowd was Dave's mum, Nan, who throughout her life was a stalwart supporter of her son's sporting prowess. In fact, she could proudly claim that both her sons went on to represent their country as Ian curled for Scotland. At Twickenham, she was one of the recipients of the two tickets provided by the Scottish Rugby Union to Dave. These were no freebies as John Law, the austere secretary of the SRU wrote in the letter informing Dave of his being awarded his "cap" that "two tickets for the match will be sent to you on receipt of remittance of £2."

Dave now back on the field, albeit with a broken nose.

The shout from the crowd which had been heard when Dave was lying unconscious was easily traced back to one of the fifty or so Howe players and members who had postponed their own club match against Perthshire Accies that weekend in order to travel to London to see their first club member play for Scotland. They were not going to let a slight injury to Dave deprive them of their enjoyment of the occasion – which also later included seeing some of the nightlife in the capital.

There may have been stars in his eyes as he regained consciousness during the match but there were no bright lights for Dave as he later recalled having to spend a long time post-match retrieving cotton wool from his broken nose.

His introduction to life as an international rugby player had started on the Friday before the match when the team met at Edinburgh Airport or as it was called in those days, Turnhouse. Following the flight down and transfer to the Hyde Park hotel which was to be their base, the team were taken to nearby playing fields where they were put through their training regimes and worked out set plays from lineouts and scrums.

Training over, it was back to the hotel. The evening saw the team being taken to one of London's theatres to see a show which the management hoped would take the players' minds off the game the following day.

While going with the flow on that first trip to London as an international player, in future trips, Dave and his long term colleague in the scrum, hooker Norman Bruce, decided a couple of beers in a quiet local pub

Dave, with his ubiquitous duffel coat, boarding the plane in Edinburgh heading for London for his first international in 1959.

was a better way of spending the evening. This was no rebellion against authority, it was just that the front row pair preferred their own method of preparation and there was no problem as long as they made sure they were back in the hotel before the other players came back from the theatre.

On match day morning the team bus, complete with a motorbike escort, took the team to a small restaurant on the side of the Thames where it was left to individuals as to whether they had a hearty lunch or just nibbled on a lettuce leaf. Dave stuck to his traditional pre-match favourite – a mushroom omelette.

Back on the bus heading to Twickenham, he had the first indication of the size of the crowd going to the match with streets full of people parting right in front of the bus just like a boat with a bow wave.

Arriving at the stadium, the tension hanging in the air was raised by the crowds of Scots fans cheering and shouting encouragement as the players got off the bus. A few of the older, more experienced ones stopped to write their names on the programmes and books the autograph hunters thrust in front of them but with the impending battle in mind, Dave just headed straight to the quiet of the dressing room.

For all the players running onto the Twickenham pitch that day, the roar of the crowd raised the adrenalin levels. For Dave, there was the wonderment from seeing the sea of faces looking down at the thirty combatants. There were lots of the proverbial butterflies in his stomach. The National Anthem of 'God Save the Queen' was played for both teams. This was long before 'Flower of Scotland' was adopted by the SRU as its anthem; a move incidentally not supported by Dave who does not like the Corries' tune. As the music played he closed his eyes and tried to concentrate on the task ahead, repeating to himself time and again that it was important not to be fazed by the occasion. He was later to state that the big difference between club rugby and internationals was the pace of the game. He adapted quickly; thus effectively ensuring for the next eight years that his name would be one of the first on the Scottish team sheet at selection meetings.

That Calcutta Cup match international was played on 21st March 1959, just six years after Dave had first picked up a rugby ball. His progress started with the Howe of Fife where his first competitive game – for the second fifteen – had taken place in October 1953. By March 1954 he had established himself in the first team at the club.

A broken ankle the following year hindered his progress as he had to withdraw from his first representative match; a game between the North of Scotland District and the Midlands District. The purpose of this trial was to pick the team to represent the wider North and Midlands area; this being one of the four rugby playing Districts into which the SRU had divided Scotland. The others were Edinburgh, Glasgow and the South.

The following year he was a member of the North and Midlands team which surprisingly achieved a resounding victory against the South. In rugby terms it was a victory on a similar scale to that achieved when David knocked out Goliath. Dave's performance that day brought him to the attention of the Scottish selectors and he was picked as a reserve for the national trial.

Injury to a leg muscle brought about by an accident in a gym once again blighted his progress in 1957/58 but he still played in the District matches that year. These included the North and Midlands against a touring Australian side in Aberdeen. The visitors won by six points to three. One reporter remarked that even though the home team pack was "out-weighed in the scrum and out-jumped in the lineouts, they made up for those shortcomings with magnificent backing up in the loose and spirited battling in the loose scrums."

His performance that day led to his being chosen for the Possibles who were the junior team to the Probables chosen by the Scottish selectors trying to decide on who best to represent the national team.

For today's full time professional rugby players, the comparison with the lifestyle of their amateur counterparts just half a century ago is hardly believable. Whether it was playing for club, district or national team,

Dave had to contribute towards ensuring the family farm was a profitable business. Throughout his rugby playing career he was an amateur in the sense of not receiving cash for his efforts. He was, however, totally professional in his approach to the game.

To ensure the farm was profitable, Dave and his brother Ian made a few changes following the death of their father in 1954. When he was growing up, the mixed arable farm had had a large flock of breeding sheep where the lambs were fattened on the farm and then sold at Cupar market. The year after their father's death, quite a number of lambs died from one of the many diseases to which sheep succumb. After digging yet another grave – on-farm sheep burial was allowed in those days – the two brothers decided that the sheep enterprise would have to be sold.

The other possible reason for the demise of the sheep enterprise was the job of fattening lambs on turnips in the depths of winter could be a very muddy, unpleasant job. The lambs had to be kept in an enclosed area to prevent them nibbling turnips right across the field thus destroying their future feed. The enclosures had wire net boundaries and when the turnips in the netted off parts of the field were completely eaten, these temporary barriers would be moved to a fresh area. Easily said but, as Dave and Ian found out in 1956, the posts holding the nets were frozen in the ground and could not be extracted. New posts were bought but it was difficult to drive them into the hard earth.

Next year, the sheep were sold.

In their place, cattle numbers were increased. This was initially through keeping more commercial or cross breeds with their calves being sold by Ian who was responsible for that part of the business. He took them to either Perth or Stirling marts – both noted for their trade in store cattle. The Rollos, being shrewd businessmen, knew that often the best profit from cattle came from selling young stock to farmers who liked to fatten animals for market.

The cattle enterprise expanded further with the introduction of a small pedigree herd of Herefords. This traditional native breed was very popular in the UK in those days and one of the big events in the farming world was the Edinburgh Hereford bull sale. It was here that Dave bought his first bull. This purchase provided the first calves for the Forret pedigree herd. The quality of his offspring was outstanding and Dave was, in the coming years, to take the best of them back to Edinburgh. The culmination of this enterprise came in 1980 when one of the Forret bulls topped the sale.

Dave and Ian with one of their champion Hereford bulls.

Going into the pedigree world is a big step and it requires knowledge of the difference between good and not so good livestock. Like generations of young farmers Dave had taken part in stock judging competitions in his youth. This sees contestants having to place livestock according to their attributes and give reasons for doing so. This training stood Dave in good stead. Soon after starting his pedigree herd, his cattle picked up prizes at agricultural shows in Perth, Kinross and Kirriemuir and on one occasion at the premier show in Scotland – the Royal Highland.

Success as an exhibitor of cattle soon found him increasingly in demand as a show judge. The job of a show judge is not enviable. It has the capacity to alienate those whose stock have not been awarded prizes while satisfying only the overall winner. Despite this reality, Dave became so respected as a judge of Hereford cattle that invitations came not just from around his home area in Scotland but also from Ireland and the heartland of the breed in England. In numerical terms, the biggest challenge he faced in placing the cattle came at Chester show where there was a very big entry of stock.

But the riskiest could have been the show he judged at Ballymena in Northern Ireland towards the end of the Troubles. While a few judges have been threatened following their decisions in peacetime, there are not too many who have had to have the police in attendance confiding quietly that this was the first show to be held following a number of fatal shootings.

By 1960, there were other livestock on Wester Forret. These were a Hunter pony and two poodles. Both had arrived as a dowry accompanying Dave's new wife, Jean.

Inevitably, the couple's first meeting had been at a rugby match in the grounds of Dollar Academy. Through its famous school the Howe had a number of connections with this town in the Hillfoots and as a result a game between Dollar Accies and the Howe was arranged. This suited Dave as he had played both alongside and against Robin Waddell from Dollar and knew him well. As team mates they had played together for the Midlands against the North and as opponents, they had already met when Dollar came through to Cupar.

The game in Dollar was well underway when Dave became aware of a slim young girl standing in a group of friends on the touchline. But due to the hurly burly of the game and the drive back to Fife after the match the memory faded . . . for the moment.

Some months passed until one night Dave's friend Andrew Adamson, who farmed at Friarton two or three miles from Forret and who also played for the Howe, suggested Dave and his then girlfriend link up with him and his new girlfriend for a night out together. The plan was to go to Kirkcaldy to a dinner dance. When they met in the hotel, Dave realised that Andrew's girlfriend was the girl who had been standing on the touchline.

Jean Waddell was a Dollar girl. Her father had a well-established butcher's shop in the town. She had attended Dollar Academy where she had distinguished herself in athletics, winning the girls' championship and going on to win at the Scottish Schools championships. Her strong events were the sprints but showing her competitive spirit, she also entered others such as the high jump and the discus in order to ensure she won the overall championship at the school.

After her school days were completed, she went off to Atholl Crescent in Edinburgh or to give its full title, Edinburgh College of Domestic Science where she did a Demonstrators' Course. This led to her being

Jean demonstrating at the Ideal Homes Exhibition, Waverley Market, Edinburgh.

employed as a Home Service Advisor for the Scottish Gas Board. Among other functions, this saw Jean doing cookery demonstrations at the Ideal Homes Exhibition at the Waverley Market in Edinburgh. In between times she could be found helping her father cook the meats he sold in his shop.

After the Kirkcaldy foursome date, Dave and Jean started seeing each other. This mostly involved Dave driving the 32 miles through to Dollar. Often the trip started by filling the car with fuel at one of the petrol stations in Cupar where the proprietor was a sweet pea enthusiast and, in season, Dave would take a bunch of these colourful and delicate flowers to his girlfriend.

Whether the flowers were critical to the blossoming of the relationship time does not relate but Jean's mother and father were both keen on this young rugby playing farmer. To ensure Dave did not go hungry on the long and winding road back to Fife, he was often presented with a pack of sandwiches by Jean's mum.

The transition from courting, as it was then called, to being a young wife on a working farm was quite a shock for Jean. Often she was called upon to help move cattle from field to field or, with greater difficulty, onto livestock floats. The farmhouse door would be flung open and she would be asked for a 'kape'. This was not a demand for rainwear but the vernacular for standing in a door or gateway to prevent the cattle from escaping into the wrong fields or sheds.

She not only 'kaped' but also coped through breeding from her two poodles, Mandy and Cindy, for whom a stud dog, Spike had been bought. With the sale of the resulting puppies Jean made enough cash to help furnish the farmhouse. To further prove she was a modern day farmer's wife Jean also brought in an income through carrying out market research on local firms for more than two decades for Produce Studies based in Newbury.

CHAPTER FIVE

INTERNATIONALS FIRST HALF

PLAYING RUGBY FOR Scotland is a battle against the odds. In rugby playing terms the country does not have the resources available to other countries. Success in Scotland comes on those occasions when there is either inspired management or a group of particularly gifted players.

Over the years from 1947 to 1999, Scotland won or shared winning the Five Nations tournament, consisting of England, France, Ireland, Wales and Scotland, a mere five times. One of the shared victories – with Wales – came in 1964 when Dave Rollo played in all four matches.

Following his first cap against England in March 1959, it was reckoned he would be an automatic pick for the Scottish team. The system in those days was to play District matches in November, then the Scottish trials in December before picking the team for the opening match of the Five Nations against France in January. The selection for the French game saw a front row of Dave alongside Norman Bruce as hooker and Hughie McLeod, as the other prop. That trio was to play thirteen internationals together and it would have been more if McLeod had not retired. Hughie, who had already toured twice with the British Lions, was a legend in the game and as a great reader of the game and a quiet advisor, he had told Dave the secret of his success was to be mobile around the field. Apart from that particularly sound advice Dave learned a great deal more from the veteran.

Against Dave in the French team that day was Alfred Roques, or the Rock as he was known. He was also a farmer but, at 15 and a half stone, he was more than a stone heavier than Dave. He was also ten years older and wise in the shenanigans that can take place in the front row of the scrum. In the years ahead the pair of them would clash on a number of occasions before Dave saw him off. In front of 60,000 spectators with at least three-quarters of that number standing in the open terraces at Murrayfield, the French won by thirteen points to eleven with the two Scottish tries scored by their captain and winger, Arthur Smith.

A trip to the national stadium in Cardiff followed for the Welsh game but again there was no success with the Scots going down by eight points to nil. It was after five minutes of this match that Dave admitted he was worried. "It was all 100 miles per hour stuff and I did not think I could last the pace." Then someone went down injured and all his interval training on the road outside the farm kicked in. "After that I never had any fear of not lasting 80 minutes. I knew the training I was doing was enough. No matter what kind of game it was – fast, slow or tough, I knew I could last 80 minutes."

Against the Irish at Lansdowne Road, newcomer Ronnie Thomson on the wing scored both Scottish tries and even though they were both unconverted they were enough to seal a victory against the five points scored by Ireland.

The 1960 Calcutta Cup game was played at Murrayfield but the home advantage was not sufficient to bring Scotland victory as they went down by twenty one points to twelve with Smith scoring the only Scottish try and full back Ken Scotland putting over three penalties. The loss consigned Scotland to the second bottom rung on the Five Nations ladder.

The trip to Paris to the opening game in the 1961 Five Nations was not the first time Dave had flown to the French capital. In 1959 Tubby Simpson, the self-appointed social convenor of the Howe of Fife rugby club, had organised a trip to see the Scotland v France match. A plane was hired and thirty bold travellers, including Dave, boarded it only to find there were no seats. Undaunted, they just hunkered down in the fuselage. All was well until one member – a farmer – decided it was all a bit stuffy and tried to open a window for some fresh air. A rugby playing career and the ownership of several thousand acres of farmland were at risk until sufficient bodies persuaded him otherwise by sitting on him.

The official Scottish team party in 1961, with Dave now an established member, was more organised and they travelled in more conventional aircraft. The outcome turned on an injury in the third minute of the game when Charlie Stewart, a farmer who played for Kelso, received a knock on his knee which badly hampered his movement. His team mates struggled on manfully and according to reporter Jock Wemyss, none more so than the front row of McLeod, Bruce and Rollo – but the end result was an eleven points to nil defeat. Dave and his colleagues in the pack received praise from the *France Soir* newspaper which reckoned the seven Scottish forwards were superior to their eight French counterparts. Little French stand-off Pierre Albaledejo scored the points, one of them a drop goal justifying his nickname of 'Monsieur le Drop'.

Two weeks later on 21st January 1961, Dave was in the Scottish team facing the South African tourists. Pre-match, the Springboks president, Danie Craven, had pointed out that his front five in the scrum had had the better of the All Blacks in a recent game and they would do the same to the Scots. However, it turned out to be a close game with the South Africans winning by twelve points to five. In his post-match interview the Boks manager Ferdie Bergh admitted that the Scots forwards had been "magnificent" and had given them a good game. For the Scots, there was consolation as they had regained some pride after being hammered 44 points to nil by the 1951 South African touring team.

A mere four days later, Dave was facing the South Africans again, this time as a member of the North and Midlands team where the invitation stipulated that players would be provided with white jerseys and red socks, but they were to bring their own white shorts. In front of a crowd of 6,000 spectators in Aberdeen, the home side went down by twenty two points to nine; a respectable result for a district team playing one of the top rugby nations. Playing in the same team as Dave that day was a speedy winger, former Bell Baxter schoolboy and Howe of Fife player by the name of David Whyte. They would meet again when both played for Scotland.

Back on Five Nations duty, Wales were next and Scotland scraped a three nil victory at Murrayfield with Rollo's contribution to the win being described as immense by respected commentator Norman Mair.

Victory over Ireland by sixteen points to eight that same month saw Rollo again being singled out by reporters for his part in the win. It also set up hopes of a Triple Crown win if the Scots could overcome the old enemy, England. The now customary theatre visit took in the musical *My Fair Lady* but it gave no good omens for Scotland as they lost six points to nil. The front row of McLeod, Bruce and Rollo were exonerated from blame but, with the absence of heavyweight Mike Campbell-Lamerton in the second row, reporters reckoned Scotland missed his "big shove".

Even if the Five Nations competition was completed as usual in March, an innovation this year saw Scotland plan a short trip to South Africa in April and May. This broke new ground for the Home Nations as it was the first trip to a rugby playing Commonwealth country. The flight out was the same lengthy route taken by the 1962 British Lions but this time the destination was Port Elizabeth where the Scots were to play a Test match against South Africa following two warm-up games against provincial teams.

The Scots were given tremendous hospitality by the many expats they met as well as by Afrikaners who knew all about rugby. As a result, Dave and his colleagues were introduced to the South African speciality of a 'braai' which is their version of a barbecue.

Dave played in one of the smaller tour matches and then lined up in the international where he played against his old adversary, Pete du Toit, whom he respected as one of the strongest props he had ever faced. After a long home season, much of it played on soft or even muddy pitches, the Scots suddenly found themselves playing on firm ground which produced quick ball. For those players making their first visit to South Africa, it was also an introduction to skin burns caused by the unforgiving ground. The Springboks triumphed by four tries, three of them converted to two converted tries or eighteen points to ten.

His performances on the rugby pitch in 1961 saw Dave nominated for the *Dundee Courier*'s McTaggart award, named after the Olympic gold medal winning boxer. Others on the short list included Bobby Cox, the Dundee Football Club captain, Jimmy Brown, Perthshire cricketer and Joyce Barclay, the Wightman Cup tennis player from Kirkcaldy. In a football dominated area, Dave did not win but he was happy that the award went to a player in his favourite football team – Dundee.

For Dave, the run up to the 1962 Five Nations was none too comfortable. His early season form had not been good and he was only selected to play in the Rest team in the final Scottish trial. However, he was not going to give up without a fight and after a sterling performance in the first forty minutes, he was promoted to the main team at half time. This, in turn, saw him selected for the French match in January where, despite being on home ground at Murrayfield, the Scots lost by eleven points to three. The newspaper reports praised the Scottish forwards and pointed to missed penalty kicks as being the main contributory factor to the failure to win. This game also marked the thirty seventh cap for his front row colleague, Hughie McLeod, who was to retire at the end of the season having won forty caps. This was a matter which would later feature in Dave's international selection.

The following month, the Scottish team were down in Wales where they recorded their first win for 35 years. Ron Glasgow, a PE teacher at Dollar Academy and Frans Ten Bos both crossed the try line and Ken Scotland converted one of those to give the Scots an eight points to three win. The pack were credited with giving the Scots their victory and there was special mention of Rollo playing like "a man possessed in his best game in a blue jersey." This performance no doubt helped his chances of being picked for the Lions tour in the summer of 1962.

Commenting on the Welsh crowds, Dave recalled how when their team was in the ascendency the noise level would rise. The opposite was true on this occasion. "We knew we had them and their supporters went quiet." Despite their famous victory, there was no welcome home for the players with a newspaper report stating "they were met by a few relatives and friends. They went unnoticed, some in cars and some in the normal service coach."

Dave missed the Irish match as a result of an injury believed to be unique among rugby players. He dropped a curling stone on his foot taking part in a Grand Match on the Lake of Mentieth. Curling is nowadays an indoor sport but its origins were on the frozen ponds and lochs. Whether it is due to global warming or some other factor, there are now years where no outdoor curling takes place. It requires a severe

Dave curling in the Grand Match. *Photo courtesy of D C Thomson* winter before a Grand Match is called as it involves more than 2,000 curlers competing on the ice. There have only been three Grand Matches in the past sixty years – in 1959, 1963 and 1979 – and Dave is one of the few people who have competed in all three. The curlers have to take their own curling stones to such an event and it was while carrying them to or from the Lake of Mentieth venue that the freak accident occurred. Dave dropped one of the curling stones weighing approximately twenty kilos on his toes.

His place in the Scottish rugby team to play Ireland was taken by his friend and fellow Fife farmer Bob Steven who previously also played for the Howe of Fife. By the time of his international call up Steven was turning out for Edinburgh Wanderers. The Scots won handsomely and Steven played his part in the sixteen points to eight victory but Dave's name was back in the frame for the England match.

With an estimated 82,500 record crowd, Murrayfield was packed. Not only was there a chance of topping the Five Nations but the selectors were present looking for candidates for the Lions tour of South Africa. This resulted in too much pressure being put on the players and at the end of a dull match, the two teams shared a three points apiece draw. Of the Scottish players who were mentioned in post-match despatches, Rollo, Smith, Campbell-Lamerton and Douglas were picked for the Lions but Glasgow missed out.

Either determined to throw off his "late starter to the season" tag or still carrying fitness honed under the South African sun, Dave roared into the Scottish trials for the 1963 Five Nations. In the first game – the Blues against the Whites – he scored the Blues' only try in their eight points to six win, thus earning the plaudits from one reporter who viewed his performance as being in a "class of its own." After the second and final trial where he played for Scotland against the Rest, he was described as being "home and dry" in earning selection.

The first game in the 1963 tournament in France was shrouded in doubt as heavy snow had fallen. Thankfully, the French had covered the pitch with straw which allowed the match to proceed. However, rather than carting the straw away before the match they burned it in the stadium. Dave recalled it was the only time he played with the acrid burning smell in his nostrils and ash on the pitch. He did not allow himself to be distracted and helped gain a notable scalp, ensuring a rare Scottish win on French soil. The final score was eleven points to nil in favour of the Scots. This was the first time in fourteen years that the French had been beaten on home soil. In doing so, he turned over his old adversary, Alfred Roques, with one reporter commenting, "Rollo had scrummaged the opposition into the ground." Roques did not take defeat easily and dismissed the traditional post-match handshake as another commentator described his actions as "departing in high dudgeon." Vivian Jenkins in the *Times* observed that Rollo had had "his best ever game in a Scottish jersey."

The Scottish performance in France seemed to augur well for the Welsh match but the men from the valleys had other ideas. Dave could thereafter state he had played in one of the most boring rugby matches ever. The Welsh tactics were based on keeping the ball tight by booting the ball into touch on every occasion and from every point on the pitch. In those days it was quite legal to do so but the sterility of the game where there were 111 lineouts in the eighty minutes caused the rule makers to introduce the touch kicking restrictions which now apply. Clive Rowlands was the Welsh skipper and he kicked his side to victory by plugging the side lines. Despite the tedium of the tactics, Dave Rollo and Norman Bruce, his hooker, were praised for their valiant efforts in a game which also included 67 set scrums. A ticket for this most boring match was £1 for the stand and one commentator reckoned it was daylight robbery.

Scotland beat Ireland in the next match by the narrow margin of three points to nil. However they were then beaten ten points to eight by England and ended up as runners-up in the Five Nations Tournament.

Rollo was described as the man of the match for Scotland which was also noted as a triumph for good running rugby. But the 'top man award' came at a cost. Dave had weighed himself after the game and was shocked to find his weight was down to 14 stones 2 pounds. Less than ninety minutes earlier he had turned the scales some six pounds heavier. It was no wonder that one commentator said Rollo played like "three men in one."

New Zealand has dominated world rugby for decades and their 1963/1964 team that toured Britain, France and Ireland did much to cement that superiority with 34 wins, one draw and one loss in their four month visit to this side of the world. Led by legendary captain,

Dave surrounded by young fans after the England game at Murrayfield.

Wilson Whineray, by the time the All Blacks arrived in Edinburgh to play Scotland in January 1964 they had already beaten Wales, Ireland and England.

Speaking prior to the Scottish match, Whineray predicted, "If we play hard, and that has been our policy throughout the tour, we will win." The All Blacks tour manager was more specific. In a reference to the comparative weights of the two teams where the visitors had a six kilos per man weight advantage over the Scots, he commented, "We in New Zealand rely on forward strength to soften up the opposition and the backs to only play a minor role." Among those providing the "forward strength" that day were Meads, Tremain and Lochore who would all go on to feature in any list of the most famous All Blacks in history.

An estimated 70,000 people packed into Murrayfield to see the match which took place thanks to the SRU's £10,000 investment in undersoil heating.

Before the match started the All Blacks went through their famous haka or war dance which is intended through gestures and moves to intimidate the opposition. "It was very impressive seeing it close up. It sort of geed me up," commented Dave who minutes later would be scrumming down against the New Zealanders who were expected to push the Scots across the park. The expected did not happen and at the end of the match neither team had scored; thus denying the visiting team a claim to have beaten all the Home Nations. The normally dependable All Blacks full back, Don Clarke, missed a couple of penalty kicks but, in an even and exciting contest, the Scots could claim they were narrowly denied a try. Describing the match, Jock Wemyss praised the Scottish pack for their "fighting spirit and remarkable stamina" in holding off their much heavier opponents.

Three weeks before the New Zealand match, Scotland had kicked off the 1964 Home Nations tournament on 4th January with a ten points to nil victory over the French at a wet and muddy Murrayfield. Dave had not originally been chosen to play as his place in the team had been taken by Brian Neill, the new Scottish captain. He was however picked as reserve and having observed the team all fit and well in the morning of the match, he had a hearty lunch. Not content with the lunch, he also had a pint of beer to help it down. After the meal, the chairman of the selectors, Charlie Drummond bought him a pint as a consolation for not playing. This was followed by Dave repaying the hospitality with another pint. A third was just being consumed when the SRU secretary dashed onto the scene saying Dave was needed to play as Cameron Boyle the Scottish loose head prop had a temperature and was not fit to play. A three course lunch and a two and a half pint preparation did not seem to faze Dave as he played his part in a ten points to nil victory as the rain poured down in one of the wettest games seen at Murrayfield. He was judged to have played well against the giant Jacques Bayerdon who was two and a half stones heavier than him.

Defeat in Cardiff by eleven points to three followed but the Scottish team rallied to beat Ireland six points to three in Dublin a fortnight later.

There was added spice to the Calcutta Cup match in 1964 as Scotland were in with a chance of topping the Five Nations if they beat England and if Wales were beaten by France. The Scots did their part of the bargain winning fifteen points to six, crossing the English try line three times; all the points were scored by forwards, Norman Bruce, Ron Glasgow and a young Jim Telfer, who would later go on to manage one of Scotland's most successful rugby teams. The 1964 win was especially sweet as this was the first Scottish victory over the Auld Enemy since 1950.

However, the Welsh squeezed a draw out of France and the championship was shared. There was a minor celebration back at the hotel. The unspoken rule seemed to be that, if Scotland had won, the team were told by the selectors to go to a certain room where they would get a black velvet – Guinness and champagne. This largesse only happened when they won. Defeat brought no such indulgence. The two teams always had a dinner in the hotel later where they mixed and the captains spoke. After the dinner a bus was laid on to take anyone who wanted to go to the Students' Union. Overnight accommodation at the hotel was available to players having to travel a distance but many of the Edinburgh or Borders based members just went home. After he was married, Dave tried to organise sharing a room with one of the local players who he knew went home. This allowed Jean to stay overnight. If that subterfuge was not possible, the pair of them just drove home.

Dave's 1964 season ended with him as a member of the first Scottish rugby team to visit Canada where they played five provincial teams; all of which yielded victories for the tourists. With so many expatriate Scots in the crowds supporting the Scottish team, Dave said this end of season tour was like playing home matches. It was very much a tour designed to develop the game in Canada and even on match days the Scottish players often spent time coaching in schools in the mornings. The tour was so tightly organised that the players were on their plane home a mere two hours after trooping off the pitch at the end of the final game.

The team was managed by Charlie Drummond, who had risen to chair the Scottish selectors after playing for Melrose. He was a banker by profession and a transfer to Cupar brought him in close contact with Dave. The under manager on the tour was Hector Monro, who was later to serve as a Scottish Minister during Margaret Thatcher's Prime Ministership. Most of the Scottish team already knew Monro either through his connections with Langholm Rugby Club or as a result of him showing the team through the House of Commons when they were down playing England in London.

CHAPTER SIX

INTERNATIONALS SECOND HALF

APART FROM HIS kilt which went with him whenever he was on international duty, another article of clothing was indelibly associated with Dave Rollo during his rugby playing days – his duffel coat. Whether the photo was of the team boarding a plane or getting off the bus heading into the stadium, there was Dave in kilt and duffel jacket. Defending his choice of clothing, Dave said the ubiquitous coat was a present from his mother at the start of his international career and it also went well with his McIntosh tartan kilt. The coat was such a trademark for Dave that when the Scottish team headed out to Paris to kick off the 1965 Five Nations tournament, one reporter noted "Rollo's duffel coat practically knew its own way to the French capital." The coat not only survived that trip, it went with him to the end of his playing career at which point he hung it up in the garage where it eventually succumbed to old age and hungry moths.

The game against France was Dave's 24th cap. By now his front row colleagues were hooker Frank Laidlaw who earned his first cap and team captain Brian Neill. The Scottish second row broke new records in both height and weight with long established Mike Campbell-Lamerton coming in at 6' 4" and 17½ stone being joined by 6'7" and 16½ stone, Peter Stagg. In today's terms when players are taller and much heavier, these statistics are not noteworthy but, in the mid 1960s, they produced a great deal of pre-match comment from reporters. To counteract the height advantage held by the Scots, the French varied their lineout and reduced the effectiveness of the two tall Scots. The French played a running game that saw them win by sixteen points to eight. Among the Scots exonerated for their performance in the game, Norman Mair in *The Scotsman* singled out Dave saying, "Rollo had another grand game." Another reporter wrote, "The Howe can be proud of Dave Rollo, he gave a brilliant display in both the tight and the loose. The way in which he worked to help his hooker's success was magnificent to see. He can look forward to his twenty fifth cap."

The post-match commentary then moved swiftly from the game to highlight the fact that the Scottish team had been to the Folies Bergère show before the match where photographs were taken of some of the players high-kicking alongside the scantily clad ladies. One of the writers wrote an article criticising this activity, saying that professional footballers would be chastised if they had behaved in this way. The following day, Norman Mair weighed in on behalf of the players describing the Folies Bergère show as "a theatre and not a den of iniquity." He must have been there to proffer this advice because he added, "the senior internationalists found the show boring and repetitive."

The Welsh game at Murrayfield was next and, with Brian Neill injured, Norman Suddon came into the front row. This provided options for change as both Suddon and Dave could play on either the tight or loose head sides of the scrum. The only other change in the Scottish team was the introduction of David Whyte who had previously made his international debut in track and field athletics. He had attended Bell Baxter and played for the Howe of Fife before heading off first to St Andrews University and then Oxford before playing for Edinburgh Wanderers from which base he won his thirteen Scottish caps. During his student days, he had won the long jump at the British athletic championships in 1959 and then gone on to represent the UK no less than nine times.

The Welsh won by fourteen points to twelve with the experts reckoning the Scots were "well beaten but not disgraced."

The reporters advised the Scottish selectors to keep the same team for the Irish match which would also be played at Murrayfield. This they did but the Scots were beaten by the Irish sixteen points to six with the Irish team being described as "too tough, fast and clever for the home team."

This brought the Scottish team to the 1965 version of the Calcutta Cup match without a single point in the Five Nations championship. The game at Twickenham ended up three points all after Andy Hancock, the English winger, scored what was described as the "try of the decade" by running the length of the pitch late on in the game and evading a few despairing Scottish tackles to touch down and level the drop goal scored by Scottish stand off David Chisholm. The Melrose player believed he had also scored a try with downward pressure being applied by him to the ball when it was over the line. Unfortunately, by the time the referee arrived, the ball had skidded away and no try was awarded.

In that game, Rollo was described as being in "rollicking form" and also "rolling back the years" in his enthusiasm for the game. He and his front row colleague, Norman Suddon, were name checked for spearheading a few "thrilling foot rushes."

Dave, second from left, leads the teams off the field at Twickenham after Scotland were narrowly defeated by England by 10 points to 8.

For his part, Dave said he found it was always difficult playing down at Twickenham. "The grounds were always a great deal firmer than they were up in Scotland and the English team were always much fitter because they had been running on top of the firm ground a bit longer than we had been in Scotland. We knew we had to work hard and we did. All the England games were close." Referring specifically to the Hancock try, he added, "We made just one mistake and he was away. If the ball had been knocked into touch, Hancock would not have made his run and we would have won that game."

Although they ended up with the Five Nations wooden spoon, the Scottish team did finish the 1965 international season on a high note, beating the South African tourists by eight points to five at Murrayfield in April. By general consensus and also by the tour statistics where they played five games and lost a similar number, this was not a good Springboks side. The Scottish scores came from a try from winger Jim Shackleton and a drop goal in the last two minutes of the game by stand-off Dave Chisholm. The forwards, with Dave in the tight head front row slot, were credited with engineering the victory. The win gave Scotland a record of being, at that time, the only Home country to have beaten South Africa not just once but twice. The win is also one of only five in the twenty five matches that have been played between the countries in the past one hundred years.

The run up to the 1966 Five Nations championship was difficult for Dave. He was only selected for the junior Whites team in the first Scottish trial; this lowly starting point possibly being linked to the North and Midlands District team having been soundly beaten by both the Edinburgh and South Districts. In fact Dave was the only player from the North Midlands to be selected for the first trial. His place in the senior team in the first trial was taken by John MacDonald of London Scottish who had had a strong start to the season. The White side were duly beaten by the Blues but Dave was described as "one of the best scrummagers on the pitch and deserving of a recall to the senior side." The selectors agreed and he featured in the final trial, playing for the

Scottish side that was beaten by The Rest – surely a most demeaning name for a team. The latter's victory was largely attributed to the goal kicking ability of the aforementioned John MacDonald.

This resulted in a front row of Rollo, Frank Laidlaw and John MacDonald lining up in the Scottish team to play France at Murrayfield in the Five Nations opener; a game that ended up three points all with David Whyte sliding over the line for the Scottish score. Whyte incidentally did not even make the first trial and only came on as a substitute in the final trial. The Scots pack dominated the game and the following day one French newspaper wrote, "The Scottish pack, a giant octopus with 10,000 tentacles, held the French by the throat. It was hell. Every French kick into touch – even if it was only to gain five yards – was a breath of air. The French were being suffocated."

One of the French players that day, Walter Spanghero, who was on the road to becoming a legend in his own country by winning fifty caps including two Five Nations championships, later listed Dave in his "Ideal World fifteen." Spanghero's testimony stated, "I have noticed his perfection in the set scrum. Unlike the exploits of some prop forwards, his are not conspicuous but in pure scrummaging, he is always there with his great strength, his formidable shove and his splendid individual technique." Spanghero, who himself was nominated by All Blacks legend Colin Meads as "the toughest opponent" he had ever played against, excluded French players from his selection composed of four New Zealanders, four South Africans, four Welshmen, two Irish and Dave. Apart from Dave, his picks for the other two in the front row were Ken Grey, New Zealand at loose head and Ken Kennedy, Ireland's hooker. It was noticeable that Spanghero did not rate the English players of his era.

The second round of the tournament saw Scotland head down to Cardiff where they played and lost eight points to three in a complete mud bath in The Arms Park. Both teams had started the match in their traditional colours of red (Wales) and blue (Scotland) but by the time the referee blew the final whistle all thirty players had acquired a uniformly mud brown strip. The Scots pack had performed well with hooker Laidlaw winning the battle in the scrum. Alongside him, Dave was described as one of the better forwards by a post-match commentator who wondered if he was "now on the wrong side of thirty (years old) along with a few of his colleagues." Another headline on the same theme was "Toss out the old boys."

However Dave was still there three weeks later as were all his other fourteen team mates when the Scots beat the Irish by eleven points to three at Lansdowne Road. The press box critics changed their tune and praised the team including all the 'old boys'.

The selectors decided to keep the winning team for the game against England but again there were pre-match questions from the press room on "how much longer DMD Rollo could continue." Mike Campbell-Lamerton was under more scrutiny but both were selected and both therefore enjoyed a six points to three victory over the Auld Enemy at Murrayfield. Almost seeming to spite those who commented on the game, both Campbell-Lamerton and Dave who played "near to his belligerent best" were singled out. Both were reckoned to have "played out of their respective skins to ensure the victory." The game was not a feast of running rugby but the Scottish diehards welcomed the result which came through a David Whyte try and a penalty from the boot of full back Colin Baikie. The win was doubly sweet for the Scots as it ensured their English visitors would collect the wooden spoon in the championship.

Outwith the rugby playing season, the summer of 1966 produced a major change to the roads infrastructure of Fife and Dundee with the opening of the Tay Road Bridge. One suggestion as to who would do the official opening produced a sporting theme. It was that 1956 Olympic boxing gold medallist, Dick McTaggart who was based in Dundee, world racing car champion Jim Clark who was born at Kilmany on the farm next door to the Rollos along with Dave should together cut the ribbon. However, the bridge opening duty went instead to the Queen Mother.

*Dave – still with number 8 – making a typical dash with ball in hand
at the North Midlands v Australia match, Aberdeen 1959.*

By 1966 Dave had represented his country against all the major rugby playing nations in the world bar one – Australia. In those days the Wallabies did not often come over to play northern hemisphere countries. Prior to their 1966/67 tour, the previous visit had been some eight years earlier where Dave had played for the North Midlands against the Wallabies. Now on 17th December 1967, the Australians were due to meet Scotland at Murrayfield; midway through the tourists' gruelling four month tour schedule.

Dave had gained a reputation for being a slow starter in the normal rugby playing season on account of harvest work taking precedence over sport. This time he was determined his name would be in the frame for the game against the travelling Aussies. This entailed the traditional route through the various stages of competition which started with his selection for a Fife Select team. With Dave as captain they played Perth and Angus. The best players in that game then represented the Midlands who played against the Highlands. Repeating the procedure, one step up, the best fifteen from that game went on to represent the North Midlands. This team then played Edinburgh in early November and recorded a rare but decisive victory over the capital's players with Dave described as being in "rampant form giving his pack a rousing lead." Making the North Midlands team performance more noteworthy was the fact that it was achieved despite losing one of their second row forwards before half time in those 'no substitute' days. Such victories against the odds come rarely and a week later it was back to reality when the North Midlands went down sixteen points to three to the all-powerful South of Scotland. Dave was reported as "fighting in a lost cause."

Perhaps it was this setback which saw him selected only for the junior side in the first Scottish trial. His team lost but one report called him a "great worker" for the losing team. The tortuous route to earning a Scottish cap continued when he was selected for a Scottish Select team. He and his colleagues in this team comprehensively defeated – by twenty three points to eight – a Combined Services team.

Dave was then selected for the full international team to play against the Aussies. This meant he had to withdraw from the match the tourists were playing against the North Midlands on the Wednesday before the big game. The Wallabies won the midweek game but lost the international by eleven points to five. On that day, the casual observer might have concluded that the swirling Murrayfield wind and an over-officious referee were the victors. However Dave was mentioned as leading the Scottish pack in a number of "rousing rushes upfield."

Perhaps because of this praise, he gained his thirty-fourth cap for the game against France in Paris in January 1967. Such had been the turnover of players, he was one of only six Scots to survive from playing the French two years previously. For once, the Scots had the good luck, although it might have been more accurate to relate that the French had the misfortune of losing one of their centres in the first half. The French did cross the try line twice but lost the game nine points to eight thanks to two penalties and a drop goal from the Scots. Despite a lot of provocation by the French, the Scots kept their cool and Dave was described as "playing with all the verve and attack of a youngster" and by another commentator as showing "that he still had the strength and the speed in those rural legs of his." Not a bad tribute for a thirty two year old.

The win in France set the Scots up well for the Welsh at Murrayfield where a storming last ten minutes by the home side resulted in an eleven points to five win.

It was after this game that Dave was asked if he was conscious of the crowd when playing in front of the estimated 70,000 spectators. "Not a lot," he replied. "You are concentrating on your own game and the person you are up against. You are trying to be on top of him all the time. You know the buzz is there. However, I did hear somebody shout 'Howe, Howe, Howe' which is the club chant and I knew I had at least one supporter. That helped to settle me down because I knew there was somebody there who knew me."

All was going well for Scotland at the top of the Five Nations Championship with games against Ireland and England still to come. But not for the first time, the Scots team fell at the Irish hurdle with injuries and enforced absences of both David Chisholm and Dave Rollo being offered up as reasons for the five points to three defeat. In Dave's case, it was very much a last minute withdrawal through tight hamstrings that saw Sandy Carmichael take to the field for his first ever cap.

Dave was fit again by the time of the English match at Twickenham in March but in a high scoring game the Scots came off decidedly second best, scoring fourteen points to England's twenty seven. One report of this match noted that "Rollo with his trademark socks around his ankles was prominent throughout." With all his playing colleagues and opposing players opting for shin pads, this most unusual aspect of Dave's playing attire had gained a number of comments over his playing years. The first one came from Jean on her first glimpse of Dave on the playing fields of Dollar. "I thought it was a bit poncy," she said but thereafter she quickly accepted the socks around the ankles were just Dave.

Then after one of his early appearances in a Scottish jersey, one of the selectors had upbraided Dave for going about the pitch wearing his socks around his ankles. With an eye for sartorial smartness, he asked, "Dave, can you not keep your socks up?" Dave replied, "I pull them up when they fall down but they are maybe more down than they are up." The selector accepted the explanation but suggested, "OK, then please yourself as long as they are up when you go onto the field." Dave commented that nobody kicked him in the shins or, at least, they did not do it more than once. Anyone brave enough to keep trying found themselves in the depths of the scrum being firmly held by Dave and being told to desist; that admonition was sufficient. That's why his socks were worn around his ankles for all the three and more decades of his playing career.

Much less visible, in fact out of sight of all spectators, Dave revealed that early on in his career he did away with wearing a jock strap which was designed to protect the testicles. Recording the fact, he said, "One day I found out I must have left mine at home. My mother must have taken it out to wash and not put it back in my kit bag. I played without it and found it made no difference. I discovered that my testicles came up inside my body. This happened when the second row came up between my legs. When they pushed against my private parts, I found after a scrum that my testicles had disappeared up inside my tummy and that was it. I reckoned I didn't need a jock strap after that!"

The 1967 Calcutta Cup match did not end Scotland's international matches that year as, in December, the All Blacks returned to these shores. Under the captaincy of Brian Lochore, they swept all before them, winning the four Test matches and being undefeated in the thirteen other games.

Scotland went down fourteen points to three in front of a 60,000 crowd at Murrayfield in a game that will forever be remembered for Colin Meads, the massive second row forward in the All Black scrum, being sent off.

With only a few minutes of the game remaining referee, Ken Kelleher, who had previously warned Meads about his behaviour, took exception to him kicking the legs from under the Scottish stand-off, Dave Chisholm. Post-match reaction to the sending off was mixed with some observers saying that he had to go while others noted that no damage had been done to Chisholm. Dave, who was playing in his thirty-seventh international, reckoned the big New Zealand farmer had been harshly dealt with. He believed there was no ill intent by Meads who had never before been sent off. The rural background of the All Blacks was emphasised, as no less than nine of their sixteen forwards on tour were farmers. Dave on the tight head side faced Ken Gray, another one of the farming fraternity, on the loose head. This was an unusual reversal of the roles they played in the 1964 three all draw when Dave was on the loose head side of the scrum and Ken was against him playing on the tight head. In conversation after the 1967 match, Dave discovered that Gray's ancestors were from Stirling. As Dave's wife Jean's family were also Grays from the Stirling area, there was a chance of more than a rugby playing link between the two front row forwards.

The 1967 All Blacks' close links to farming were to see their tour curtailed because large areas of Britain were suffering from foot and mouth disease. The international against Ireland was cancelled thus robbing the all-conquering team of the opportunity to complete a Grand Slam of victories. The possibility of transmitting the highly virulent disease back to their home country where the economy is based on agriculture also saw the All Blacks burning their kit at the end of the tour.

Inevitably Dave's route into the 1968 Scottish team was peppered with question marks as to how much longer he could represent his country. By now the press had cottoned on to the fact that he was the oldest player in the Scottish squad. This brought him under their scrutiny. Prior to the final trial, Norman Mair wrote, "there is much apprehension regarding the current soundness, not of wind but of limb, of the endlessly reliable D M D Rollo" but then in a later article by the same respected rugby reporter, Dave was said to be in "rampant form."

Paradoxically for those predicting the end of his international career, there was also speculation as to whether Dave could beat the record number of Scottish caps held by Hughie McLeod. The reckoning was that if he played in all four internationals he would end up with forty one caps; thus beating McLeod's forty.

Typical of the man, Dave Rollo commented on neither piece of reportage, restricting his views to the prospects in the next match or, when pressed, his ambitions for his Herefords at the next bull sales.

Cap number thirty-eight came in the home game against the French which the visitors won by eight points to six. Scottish fingers were pointed at missed goal kicking opportunities. With the exception of props Sandy Carmichael and Dave, the rest of the defeated home pack were criticised for coming off second best. Dave's performance was described as "getting through a power of work."

Despite the defeat by the French, the selectors kept faith with the team that went down to Cardiff to play Wales. The Welsh won by five points to nil and also provided the star player in Gareth Edwards who, although only twenty years old, was captaining his side. The Welsh forwards also dominated with only the Scottish front row of Carmichael, Laidlaw and Dave getting positive reviews; Carmichael for "some inspired bursts," Laidlaw for sharing the hooking spoils and Dave "for some splendid work."

The typewriter critics went into full flow and called for changes to be made. Whether the selectors listened or not is difficult to tell but three newcomers came into the Scottish side to play Ireland. The Scots front row was retained and this brought Dave up to forty caps, thus equalling McLeod's record. The changes made no difference to the outcome as the Irish overran the Scots by fourteen points to six with the Scottish scores coming from two penalties by Stewart Wilson.

Lying at the bottom of the Five Nations table with no points and with only the English match to come, the clamour for change in the Scottish team grew among the press corps. At the same time, the first hints of a conspiracy against Dave getting the record started appearing in the press. The theory was that the selectors could not see a representative from a provincial club, such as the Howe of Fife, holding the record thus beating players from the strongholds of Scottish rugby – Edinburgh and the Borders. Dave kept quiet and did not comment. Then he received a phone call from Charlie Drummond, convenor of the selectors to say, "We have selected you for the next match." That night in the Rollo household, there was quiet jubilation at Dave, once again, being chosen to play for Scotland. However, when the newspapers came out two days later, he searched in vain to see his name in the team list. He and five others who played against Ireland were dropped. Drummond phoned to say there had been a reconvened meeting and one or two of his colleagues had changed their minds.

Norman Mair of *The Scotsman* commenting on Dave's non selection, said, "The whole of Fife and further North believe that the selectors never intended to allow a player from a so called 'unfashionable club' to take away from the mighty Hughie McLeod's record in the matter of caps. Elsewhere others insist that authority has bent over backwards to accommodate (the selection of) the Fife farmer. Myself, I consider they (the selectors) have endeavoured to judge him strictly on his merits and that had Scotland performed more successfully against Wales and Ireland last year Rollo would have had his 41st cap against England."

The *Courier* rugby reporter called the decision to drop Rollo "certainly curious and almost inexplicable."

As a travelling reserve sitting in the grandstand at the match, Dave took no joy in seeing the new look Scottish team succumb to the English by eight points to six thus anchoring them firmly to the foot of the Five Nations table that year and being awarded the proverbial wooden spoon. Neither did he get any enjoyment from an 'outraged Rollo supporter' slipping a replica of the wooden spoon through the door of Charlie Drummond's house.

Quietly he thought he would do his utmost to get back into the international frame next season.

CHAPTER SEVEN

HANGING UP HIS BOOTS

IN TERMS OF weather, the 1968 summer was better than average. That meant a great deal to Dave and his brother Ian as even marginally better weather is important to those who grow crops in Scotland. Not only does warmer, drier weather bring the harvest earlier, it also reduces the sheer physical effort it takes in the busiest season of the year. Throughout his playing career, Dave was saddled with the reputation of being a late starter in the rugby playing calendar. Much of this related to whether his fields of grain had been cut and cleared or if they still stood in the field waiting for the weather to improve before being harvested.

The earlier than normal 1968 harvest was therefore a bonus for Dave who was determined to return to the international scene after being dropped for the English match at the tail end of the previous season. His determination to represent Scotland did not have much to do with the rugby commentators' obsession with the possibility of Dave breaking the record for the number of caps awarded to a Scottish rugby player. It was all to do with Dave's own assessment of his ability to compete at the highest level.

He started the season well, playing his way through the North Midlands district matches and was selected for the Scottish trial games where he first played against Ian McLaughlan who was later to captain Scotland. "This was the first time I came across anyone I felt was a bit stronger than myself," Dave admitted afterwards. In that final trial match he was playing for the junior team, and reporter Norman Mair said Rollo showed he was still up to international standard. He was described by another reporter as "still being lively." Despite the junior team winning the trial by nineteen points to eleven, when the Scottish team was announced, Dave's name was not on the sheet.

"I was selected as a travelling reserve for the first game which was over in Paris. Whether it was the SRU saying thank you for my past by taking me over for a trip to France, or whether they wanted cover for both props, I do not know. However I quite enjoyed that day."

Although he was not to turnout for Scotland again he was far from finished with rugby and the quality of his play was such that his non-selection continued to be debated by the press for a number of years.

In one example, the Cupar based *Fife News* carried a view which asked, "Are the Scottish rugby selectors deliberately trying to prevent Dave Rollo gaining his 41st International Cap? Is there someone amongst them who cannot stand the thought of a member of one of Scotland's minor clubs becoming the holder of a fine record?" These rhetorical questions were raised at the exclusion of the Howe of Fife's forward from the Scottish team to play Australia at Murrayfield on Saturday 2nd November 1968.

The newspaper article continued, "When Scotland lost to England in the Calcutta Cup match back in March, it was the general opinion that without Dave Rollo the Scottish team's front row scrummaging had no plan, no opening moves and no sustained power. If Dave had played in that match he would have been a certainty for the British Lions team which toured Africa this past Summer (1968)."

In another newspaper, Ian Cameron in the *Scotsman* said that prop forwards, like old soldiers never died, especially if they were Fife farmers. "Dave Rollo, whose omission from last year's Calcutta Cup team, after equalising the Scottish record of 40 caps, causing a wave of indignation, is having another go."

While he did miss out on selection for the Scottish team to play the 1968 Australian tourists, Dave was given the honour and responsibility of captaining the Scottish Districts select team that faced the Aussies in the midweek game before the international.

The clamour for Dave to come back into the national team continued into the spring of 1969 when, after Scotland were beaten seventeen points to three by Wales, the *Courier's* rugby correspondent wondered whether this would be a way back for Dave getting in the team. Meanwhile Bruce Lewis in the *Daily Express* wondered whether the selectors would consider "bringing back Rollo as prop by moving Sandy Carmichael (then playing in the front row) to the second."

Later that season Dave and Ian McRae, from Gordonians, were the only two international players to represent the North of Scotland squad which played the South African touring team. Some eight years earlier the same pair had played at the same Linksfield pitch in Aberdeen against the 1961 touring Springboks where the match programme described them both as "battle scarred". The North were crushed by the tourists that day but four days later the full Scottish team beat South Africa at Murrayfield. Many of the games in that 1969/70 tour were affected by anti-apartheid demonstrations where politicians such as Gordon Brown, Peter Hain and David Steel played a prominent role.

Although not featuring in the Scottish team, Dave's playing diary was kept full between turning out for his club, Howe of Fife and receiving an unrivalled list of invitations to appear in famous teams such as the Barbarians, the Irish Wolfhounds and the Co-optimists.

Between 1960 and 1970, Dave played fourteen times for the Barbarians or Baa Baas as they are colloquially called. Twice he captained them and twice he crossed the try line in the distinctive black and white hooped Barbarians jersey but Dave's links with this invitational team, famed for its open free style rugby, also included a little off-field activity. In November 1962 the Barbarians, with Dave prominent in the scrum, had ground out a hard fought three all draw with a Canadian touring side at Gosforth. After the match the Barbarians trooped out to their team bus which was due to take them back to their hotel. There was only one snag

– the driver was not to be seen. After waiting for some time, Dave's team mates persuaded him to drive the bus. Used to driving various machines on his farm, driving a bus was no problem and soon the vehicle with Dave behind the wheel was heading down the motorway. It was at this point a police car went past with its siren screaming and its blue light rotating like a dervish. Dave pulled into the nearest layby and swiftly vacated the driver's seat. Entering the bus, the police were surprised to find no driver and initially no one admitting to driving. But the threat of arresting the whole Barbarians team soon saw Dave admitting guilt. He was charged with taking away and driving a bus without a licence or insurance and was told to appear in the local magistrates' court the following Monday.

This saw him travel by train from home to Newcastle on the due day and sit among the petty criminals and prostitutes; all of whom were up for various minor offences. Dave's lawyer, Gordon McKeag, pleaded in mitigation for his client that he had "fallen into a spirit of infectious gaiety and driven the bus away." McKeag added that there was no suggestion of drink having been taken and noted that the bus had been "perfectly driven." Showing little leniency, the magistrate fined Dave £10 for taking the bus away, £5 for not having a bus driver's licence and £25 for having no insurance. He was also banned from driving for six months. At the time of the arrest his team mates had assured Dave they would chip in to pay any fine but that promise to recompense him has never yet materialised.

His first game for the Barbarians came in March 1960 when one of his team mates was the legendary Irishman, Tony O'Reilly. Illustrating his longevity at the top, Dave's final appearance for the Barbarians came a decade later in April 1970 by which time he had played his final international for Scotland.

With his free running style of rugby, Dave was also a favourite choice with the Scottish Co-optimists side and, in 1962, he took part in a sixty points to three demolition of the Edinburgh University team; the biggest winning margin by the Co-optimists since they were founded in 1924. Four years later, he again took part against the same opponents and he was reported as being a "man on a mission" – his target being the retention of his place in the Scottish team. In November 1970, Dave was instrumental in getting a Co-optimists team to come to Cupar where they celebrated the introduction of floodlights on the first fifteen pitch.

Chief Constable Willie Merrilees presents the Murrayfield Sevens Cup to Co-optimists' captain Tony O'Reilly. Players from L to R: Arthur Smith (partially obscured), Dave, Phil Horrocks-Taylor, Jock Steven, Ronnie Dawson and Andy Mulligan.

The Co-optimists also gave him his biggest triumph in the shortened version of the game – seven-a-side rugby. He had played sevens for the Howe almost from the start as one of the prerequisites of the game is to have mobile forwards and Dave was mobile. Back in 1957 he was one of the Howe sevens team that lifted the Midlands trophy. His ability to run around the field in the full fifteen-a-side game was also identified by the Co-optimists when they picked a star studded team to contest the 1960 Murrayfield sevens. The illustrious other six were Tony O'Reilly, Andy

Mulligan and Ronnie Dawson from Ireland, English international, Phil Horrocks-Taylor, Hamish Kemp, from Scotland and Arthur Smith, Scottish captain. Apart from Kemp, all of them were also British Lions. There was a late change to the Co-optimists team when Kemp called off and his place being taken by Jock Steven from Madras club. Not surprisingly, this team of top stars won handsomely and Dave considered the day's efforts to have been "good fun."

His links with the Irish were strengthened through being invited to play for the Irish Wolfhounds. Again this was an invitational side based on playing open rugby and they drew their team from all the Five Nations countries. His first invitation to play for the Wolfhounds came prior to his international debut. It involved flying over to Belfast to play against Ulster. This was his first visit to the Emerald Isle and it was also his first meeting with Harry McGibbon who was later to be assistant team manager with the British Lions in South Africa. Dave relished the experience. "I enjoyed meeting the people over in Ireland and I enjoyed playing their (the Wolfhounds) style of rugby."

That game in 1957 was the first in quite a number in which he played for the side with most of the rest being against the big teams in England such as Leicester, Harlequins and Northampton. The Wolfhounds also played against Oxford and Cambridge Universities.

Looking back on these trips, Dave said that most games took place mid-week and involved a maximum of thirty six hours away from the farm. "I used to get the overnight sleeper train from Cupar to London and the next morning, I would travel to where the game was being played. After the match it was back for the sleeper that evening. The train would get into Cupar at about seven in the morning so I was ready to work.

"I suppose I was fortunate, I was in a job where I could get away as easily as I did but I always had to catch up with the work when I came home."

Throughout his career, Dave continued to play for the Howe of Fife whenever he could. He captained the first fifteen on two occasions.

Dave, centre front, captaining Howe of Fife first XV in the 1960s.

The first time was the 1961/62 season and this was followed up with a five year stint from 1965 to 1970. Throughout his captaincy, he was also turning out for the Scottish national team and had to miss a few matches but he was considered such an inspirational leader when he was playing that the Howe hierarchy decided he had to be allowed to go and represent his country on other occasions.

Even after standing down as club captain of Howe first fifteen, Dave continued playing and passing on his knowledge of the game to younger players. He played two years with the second fifteen and then followed this with three years with the thirds. It was during this final phase in his playing days that the *Courier* picked up on the success of the third choice team. "Coached and captained by Dave Rollo, the Howe thirds' last three matches have produced a points total of two hundred and seventy three for with three against." Commenting on the statistics, Dave expressed concern over the defensive lapse that allowed the opposition to score a try! Later that same season a tongue in cheek report on a game against Aberdeen University, when Dave scored one of his rare tries, stated, "Rollo shows promise." He was thirty nine years old at the time.

He officially hung up his boots in 1978, aged forty four after a quarter of a century of playing at all levels of the game. In an interview conducted in 1960, he had indicated he might retire when he reached thirty years old. He well exceeded his original prediction.

As it happened, he never left the game, as he was soon enticed into coaching. There were several triggers for this move. Possibly the prime one was, in his words, "When I was captain of the junior sides at the club, I thoroughly enjoyed seeing the youngsters coming through and I thought I could help them with my experience." It was also the time when PE teachers largely withdrew from overseeing Saturday schoolboy games and this left a gap in introducing the next generation to the game.

Another reason for his move into coaching was simple. "I liked rugby so much I thought I might be able to help a wee bit." To ensure he was up to speed on the coaching front, he attended courses at Troon and Edinburgh and these, combined with his own experience, soon provided results.

He was one of the Howe coaches who, in the 1980s, steered a youth team to Murrayfield for the Digital Youth Cup, where they just lost out to a team from Hawick. "That was a great achievement and I felt there were players in that team who could have gone on to play for Scotland."

With his playing career at an end what he wanted most of all was to see the next generation take over.

CHAPTER EIGHT

A SECOND SPORTING ROLLO

WHEN HE DECIDED to hang up his rugby boots, one reason Dave gave for doing so was because he wanted to devote more time to helping his daughter, Pat in her sporting endeavours. She had inherited sporting genes both from her father and her mother who had been a schools sports champion. In addition, she possessed a steely determination to win, with the net result that she ended up by representing both Scotland and Great Britain more than a dozen times in track and field competitions. In the course of her career, she set Scottish National and Native records for her event; the 100 metre hurdles. These record times of 13.35 seconds and 13.51 seconds respectively still stand today; a third of a century after they were set making them among the oldest in the record books.

Being brought up on the family farm, Pat's early interest was not in athletics but in horses. Her mother was keen on breeding horses and she encouraged Pat into becoming involved in pony club events and horse showing. She was successful and the family album has many photographs of Pat and a variety of ponies, complete with winning rosettes. Part of the preparation for those events saw the garden at home complete with horse jumps and Pat remembers that when she was not on her pony she used to hurdle over these jumps; an early start to her international athletics career.

In similar fashion to many other youngsters who have gone on to excel in sport, business or academia, it was an inspirational teacher who lit the imagination and encouraged the development of her athletic talent. In Pat's case, the push into athletics came from Janette Webster, her PE teacher. That encouragement and her inbuilt talent, as she had no training other than at school, saw Pat win a Bronze Medal in the under fifteen year old age category 75 metres hurdles at the Scottish Schools Championship in 1975 before improving to take the Gold Medal in 1976 in the same event.

At this stage in her athletics career, Pat did not specialise in one event. Instead she tried and enjoyed others, including competing in a pentathlon which covered five disciplines – 200 metres sprint, high jump, long jump, shot put and hurdles. She did well in those events and became Scottish Schools Senior Pentathlon Champion in 1979; this success coming despite the 200 metres being changed to an 800 metres race. But it was obvious her best chance of greater success would come through specialising in the hurdles where she seemed to have a natural talent. Looking back on her career she admits that even when she wasn't that good at school she always seemed to know she could be. "It didn't occur to me that I couldn't be good. I don't know whether it was because dad was already a Scottish international. It didn't seem a big deal."

Although she did no specific training for her event during the winter when she played hockey, Pat was hopeful that 1977 would bring more success in the next age group. Sadly, at the Scottish Schools Easter training camp she tore her cruciate ligament in her knee and after a visit to a specialist was told she would probably never run again. At this low point, her father Dave suggested that the pair of them would, through an intermediary, get in touch with the physiotherapist at Dundee Football Club, Eric Ferguson.

Dave had earlier in his career suffered damage to his knee and the injury had been treated by Ferguson, who was also the Scottish football physiotherapist at the time. It was with some trepidation that the fifteen year old girl hobbled in to see this man whose verdict would be so important. "He told me, 'no problem. I will have you back on your feet and running in about six months.' That was a big, big moment for me as, by that time, I believed I could do well in athletics," recalled Pat. The knee repair work was neither easy nor straightforward. It required extensive work by Ferguson but soon he wanted to see how Pat could cope with hurdles. In what was probably a first for the Dens Park football ground, hurdles were placed out on the grass so that a check could be made on Pat's progress. As it was, Ferguson was as good as his prediction and although Pat lost a season's athletics, she was back on track in 1978 where she went on to win the Scottish Under 17 age group 80 metre Hurdles Championships. This success saw her selected to represent Scotland in the British Schools International; all of this was achieved in what is considered to be one of the more technical athletic events and it was achieved with neither winter nor specialist training.

Her obvious, but still raw talent was picked up by the Scottish Women's Amateur Athletics Association selectors who enquired if Pat had ever competed over the slightly longer 100 metres hurdles. The reason behind the query was because the SWAAA wanted Pat to run for Scotland in an international for under twenty year olds. She was only sixteen years old at this time and had never tried the longer distance. "I borrowed hurdles from the school and put them in the back garden at the farm. I tried the first three hurdles and thought, 'I can do this.' I then went down to the artificial track at Glenrothes and repeated the experiment which again went well." This was her first international appearance and she came in third despite never previously having run the full race. Her time of 14.9 seconds put her ninth in the Senior Rankings in Scotland that year.

During her final year at school, Pat won the Scottish Schools Over 17 year age group 100 metre hurdles, as well as the pentathlon. And then in September she was off to Dunfermline College of Physical Education to prepare for a career teaching physical education. As is often the case with young sportsmen and women the transition from school to college/ university can be difficult. During that first year Pat found that there were many distractions which prevented her from making progress in her athletics career. However, her second winter at college coincided with her working with her first specialist coach, Ron Smith and their training sessions took place either at Caird Park in Dundee where he lived or in Edinburgh where she was studying.

By the spring of the following year, Pat's times started to come down significantly and at the end of the summer she was selected to compete in an international track and field event in Norway. The excitement of receiving the invitation was tempered a little by the details spelled out in those days of amateur athletes. Pat was informed that Scottish internationalists were allowed one Scottish vest every three years but they had to provide their own white shorts and tracksuits had to be bought.

At this stage in her life she had never been abroad, nor had she ever flown. Travelling to compete for your country may sound glamorous but Pat did not find it so, as neither the accommodation nor the food was particularly good. She consoled herself with the thought that it made her quite resilient. She did not know it at the time but her experiences on this trip abroad, and others that were to follow, would be put to use in the future when she became an athletics team manager. The Norwegian trip also brought home to her the different approach she needed for her event when competing abroad. Pat said, "When you are competing at home everything revolves around your one event. You travel when you want and you have your meals when it suits. Whereas when you are on an international trip and the team travels together, the bus leaves the hotel at a certain time and you have to get on that bus whether you are competing in the first or last event."

Pat was too young to remember her father playing for Scotland. She was only six years old when he won his fortieth and final cap and at that young age did not realise the significance of the game. But with the generations changed and Pat progressing in her sport, Dave was always on hand to offer advice. Often it was just a calming or comforting word. Sometimes it was just the quiet empathy of knowing when not to say anything. The important point being he was on hand if needed. When she

Father & daughter

was training, Dave was sure she would have been a much better hurdler
if she had followed his suggestions. Much though she appreciated her
dad's presence, she needed a specialist athletics coach and in Ron Smith
she had found one. With him offering specialist routines and working
on her hurdling technique right round the calendar year, her times came
down dramatically over the following two years.

Due to this more intensive training, Pat started to be invited to some of
the big international events held at Crystal Palace where the competition
was of a UK national standard. Initially she looked on in awe at British
record holders and other stars brought in from abroad by the organisers.
Pat admitted to being a trifle intimidated by some but that phase soon
wore off as she proved she was up there with the best.

With this progress, Pat and her coach made a long term plan whereby

Pat well ahead of the rest of the field at the Scottish Championships in 1983.

the main target would be representing Scotland at the Commonwealth Games in Brisbane in late 1982. The first objective was to win the SWAAA championships earlier in the year. This she duly did by beating Margot Wells, the wife of Allan Wells the Olympic Gold medal winning sprinter, and Ann Girvan, an aspiring youngster. The Scottish record holder, Elaine McMaster was absent from that race.

Pat's victory was followed by a successful summer season so that by the time the selectors sat down to pick the team for Australia, the newspaper pundits were tipping her as a cert. However, when the Scottish team was announced, the chosen competitors were McMaster and Girvan with Wells as travelling reserve. There was outrage in the papers but, having experienced the vagaries of selection himself, Dave advised Pat "to pick yourself up and show they can't afford not to select you." Days after the announcement was made, Pat took her dad's advice and turned in a top performance at the Highland Games in Edinburgh where she broke the Scottish National and Native records. Her time that day placed her fourth best in the Commonwealth in her event but even this did not produce a change of heart by the selectors. While she did not comment publicly on the non-selection, her coach Ron Smith stated categorically that "the selectors had made a mistake and Pat would have won a medal."

The next step up the athletics ladder came closer to home with the UK championships at Meadowbank in 1983. Pat finished a close second to the British record holder, Shirley Strong and this led to her being awarded her first British vest for the match against Russia or the Soviet Union as it was then called. Pat's second place at Meadowbank also

Pat leading Sally Gunnell over the hurdles at Meadowbank against Russia.

produced a new Scottish National and Native record of 13.51 seconds and, continuing her good form, she came within fractions of a second of that time in fourth position against the Russians.

A whole series of international invitations followed that summer during which she also completed her final year at college. She was selected for the British team to go to the World Student Games in Canada. But to make the team plane, she had to change her clothes on the way as she was rushed straight from her graduation in her parents' car.

She broke the Scottish record at the Games which were held in Edmonton although she missed out on making the final. But her whirlwind summer continued when she posted a time of 13.35 seconds on her return to the UK at the WAAA Championships. This was better than the qualifying time set for the event at the World Championships in Helsinki, but came a day after the selection date, so once again Pat missed out on selection causing her to be labelled by one of the sports writers as the 'unluckiest athlete.'

1984 was an Olympic year and Pat started off well as the only Scottish winner at the UK championships held in Wales that year. There was tight security around the stadium on account of anti-apartheid protests against the presence of Zola Budd, a South African born but British registered athlete. Pat's winning time of 13.12 seconds was her fastest ever but it does not feature in the record books because it was wind assisted, although it did stand as a Championship Best Performance. More importantly, in winning, she beat two other candidates vying for Olympic selection.

By the time of the trials for the Los Angeles Olympics, Pat was working as a full time teacher, often carrying out extra-curricular duties after the school day. Then it would be a dash over to Dundee for a three hour training session. Sometimes, she would do additional training at lunchtime so she could fit in a twice a day schedule. Apart from being super fit, she was also, at the end of the school year, absolutely exhausted. In comparison with the technical support top athletes have nowadays, hers hardly existed. Pat recalled, "I was still in contact with the physio at Dundee football club but other than that I had no access to dieticians, strength and conditioning coaching expertise, sports psychologists or lottery funding."

In the Olympic Trials, Pat came third behind Shirley Strong – then UK champion – and a British athlete who was based in America. The trial decided who was to be in the British team. Her time was well within the qualifying requirement but again she missed out on selection.

Weeks later she smashed the opposition in the Scottish championships winning in 13.26 seconds and, in doing so, in the words of one well known commentator, "emphasised the injustice of her non selection." Shirley Strong took the silver medal in the Games and, while times and events should not be compared, Pat's 13.26 seconds would have placed her fifth in the final.

Although disappointed at missing out on the Los Angeles Games, she had some consolation in the large number of late season invitations to major track and field events both at home and abroad.

The following season there were no major Games and there were few highlights although Pat competed in more internationals. She tore her hamstring at the end of the year and this was a major worry. Athletes' eyes were already on the Commonwealth Games that were due to come back to Edinburgh in 1986. As it turned out, politics dominated these Games. Many of the African countries boycotted them as a result of the UK Government insisting on keeping sporting links with South Africa which was still in an era of apartheid.

The Games went ahead but Pat had been unable to train through the winter because of her hamstring injury, which had also led to a back problem which continued to hinder her progress. In the run up to the Games, she had managed to do two or three months' training. This was sufficient to get into the team but not having put in the real hard training, she did not make it into the final. She was, as she said at the time, "hugely, hugely disappointed."

Describing the position she found herself in, she said, "Being in front of the home crowd was more difficult for me that year because I wasn't totally fit and I wasn't confident I was going to be able to do my best. That was probably the most disappointing thing." Sally Gunnell, who would six years later win gold at the Barcelona Olympics, won the 100 metre hurdles but her time, admittedly on a cold Scottish summer day, was 13.29 seconds; slower than Pat had achieved two years earlier.

A light training session after these Games brought her sporting career to an end but not an end to her interest in athletics. Recalling the moment, Pat said, "I was on the beach and it was actually like I had been shot in the back as it went into a spasm. It was a good job mum had come along with the dog because I couldn't drive, couldn't do anything." She saw various specialists and was told she could have had an operation on her lower back but there was no guarantee it would be successful. There was also a worry that her teaching job might be jeopardised if the operation did not work. While Dave was active in his chosen sport up until he was fifty years old, Pat retired at 25 although she did make a brief reappearance at the end of the 1990s competing in 100 and 200 metre flat races for local club Fife AC in League matches. She then went on to win three events at the Scottish Veterans Championships in the year 2000.

Still wanting to be involved in athletics, Pat started coaching the next generation and soon proved her ability in this field by bringing two of her protégées up to Scottish selection in her own event; the hurdles. However, because of the time commitment that coaching needed, she decided not to go further. Explaining her decision she stated, "To coach at the level I would have wanted to be at, would have meant going back to two or three hours a night, maybe for four or five days a week and it was also too similar to my day job."

Another option for continued involvement in athletics came along in 1998, when she was part of the team managing the Scottish Schools team at an international event. The governing body for athletics was looking

Pat, first left, with the Scottish Schools team at the
World Gymnasiade in Caen, France in 2002.

for someone to manage their teams and because of her own experience,
Pat was ideal for the job. Initially her responsibilities were at junior level
but she soon moved on to looking after senior Scottish teams.

"It was good because I could empathise with the athletes as to what
they were feeling because, having competed myself, I was probably in a
better place than most to understand," she reflected.

She assumed that managing athletics teams would be basically
similar to some of her teaching duties but soon found out she had to
go through quite a learning curve. Not only had she to deal with the
athletes but she had also to work with their coaches, many of whom
could be extremely single-minded. There were many other trials and
tribulations for a team manager taking a group of people abroad.
Explaining this, she said, "It is not like managing hockey or rugby
teams where everybody went to play in a particular game. Athletes
are all individuals with differing demands and they bring along their

coaches while the younger ones have their parents. All of these together need careful management."

She recalled that some of the accommodation was less than wonderful with one hotel in Greece which had been re-opened for the team marked out for special comment. There were no sheets for the beds. In fact there were no slats for the beds. What was not in short supply were bugs – lots and lot of them and all the insects were mightily annoyed at being disturbed.

Athletics team managers also have to ensure all equipment travels with the team. Mostly this is no big problem but items such as fibreglass vaulting poles were troublesome. "They were often really difficult because they didn't always fit into buses. Neither did they fit into some planes. One airline actually asked if they could cut them in half to get them in!" she recalled. "Sometimes the poles which can be up to five metres long didn't appear at their intended destination because they had been put up on a different plane. Making sure all the necessary equipment was in the right place at the right time was a real issue."

However, she not only coped with the many new hurdles placed in her team management path, she successfully cleared them. The governing authorities recognised her abilities in looking after squads of youngsters and, as a result, she managed teams of athletes for the next decade including looking after the Scottish team at two Youth Commonwealth Games. The first in 2000 was on home territory, being in Edinburgh. This was followed by another similar appointment in Bendigo, Australia in 2004.

She was then awarded the post of athletics team manager or team leader for the Commonwealth Games in Delhi. This was a major commitment with preparatory work starting two years before the event itself. This often saw Pat juggling her full time job with meetings in the evenings and at weekends. It was essential that all potential athletes and their coaches were kept informed about training facilities, accommodation and all the other matters of importance to modern sportspeople.

Once out in Delhi, the work was intensive with eighteen hour days being put in by the management team. Just as there was a gulf between what her dad received in player support and the wraparound attention present day rugby players have, her management experiences drove home to Pat the developments in managing athletes from her own competition days.

She explained, "Now there is so much more available as a result of better funding. For example, leading athletes have their physio fees covered. If I was competing now at the level I was then, I would have a physio and medical back-up to try to prevent my injuries happening."

In Delhi, apart from doctors and physios, there were also communications people giving athletes media training. But Pat never thought about that. She was often picked out for interview because of her dad's achievements.

Her work back at Bell Baxter School was also expanded after she was appointed a Sports Coordinator and this, as it turned out, helped fulfil one of her dad's dearest wishes. The job entailed encouraging youngsters into sports competitions that the school did not provide. Through the enthusiasm of one of the stalwarts of the Howe of Fife Rugby Club, Russell Ferguson and Pat's new role in expanding participation in sport, links were made between the school and the club. As a result, Bell Baxter entered the Scottish Schools Rugby Cup. The school did reasonably well in the competition up until 2007 when a team came along that was totally focussed on winning the cup.

Describing the progress this team made, she commented, "At the beginning of the year we went to the Scottish Schools sevens at Murrayfield where Bell Baxter won. On the bus home, the chat was that that this was the first step to winning the Schools Cup. The players were totally matter of fact about it. It wasn't a pipe dream. Their coaches, Gary Horne and John Lathangie had drilled into them they could go all the way."

As team manager, Pat had all the organising to do, both with the other competing schools and the Scottish Rugby Union. The first round saw the school team travel to Wick where they won handsomely. The team progressed and, as it did so, the size of the local following swelled.

Dave presenting the Scottish Schools Cup to Chris Mason, captain of Bell Baxter first fifteen.

Among the crowd was Dave Rollo. He was seeing one of his dreams come true. Bell Baxter and the Howe of Fife were producing another generation of top class players.

The final was played against Dollar Academy at Murrayfield which left the Rollo household with a minor dilemma as Jean was a former pupil at the school.

Prior to the match, the school teams had been asked if they wanted to bring their school pipe bands along. This well-intentioned query was based on the premise that most of the public schools in Scotland had a pipe band and all the previous winners of the cup had come from public schools. Bell Baxter had no pipe band but they did have a samba band and when they won, their own samba music filled the stadium. No one in the big crowd at the match was more pleased than Dave. This was where he had played some of his best games and he was there to see another generation play the open running game he loved. Pat turned a blind eye to her father handing the boys a bottle of champagne to celebrate their victory.

CHAPTER NINE

TRIBUTES AND ANECDOTES

DAVE HAS SPENT more than sixty years playing and following rugby. In that time, he has not only scrummaged with the best of them but has also enjoyed their company off the field of play.

The following is a collection of comments and anecdotes from some of his friends and colleagues.

Ian McLauchlan was universally known as the Mighty Mouse on account of his relatively short stature – five foot nine and a half inches – and his being as broad as the proverbial barn door. He captained Scotland through one of its more successful phases and played in eight Lions Tests, only once ending up on the losing side.

Rarely in life do you meet a person who is universally liked and respected. For this to be someone who has played a very physical sport at the very highest level is probably unique but such is the case with Dave Rollo. I have never heard anything but good of the man.

I admire him because he has no airs or graces and he also tends to see the better things in people or in the modern game of rugby which is, of course, so much different to the game that he excelled in.

Last year (2015), in Ireland after the international, it was wonderful to see Dave with the Irish trio of Syd Millar, Tom Keirnan and Ronnie Dawson, all 1962 Lions tourists, giggling like schoolboys as they recounted tales of the past in which they were probably involved. Rugby friendships never fade with the passing of time.

Jordanhill, my club, played Howe of Fife, Dave's club, early in the season. It was invariably a fair old tussle which I looked forward to. Dave was a fair and honest player who always tested his opponent to the end of the game. We also met when Glasgow met the North and Midlands in the Inter District championship. This was a big step up from club rugby but again a great test against Dave.

Early in my career I played with Dave in an international trial at Murrayfield. It was a wet, dreich day in early January. In the dressing room Dave was plastering himself with embrocation and he asked me to help him apply it to his shoulders and back. Being a naïve college boy I enquired about this substance and its advantages. "It's coo liniment and it keeps you warm and relaxes your muscles. Try it." So I rubbed this stuff all over my body. It was fine and felt good until we went into the field but as soon as the wet touched my body it went on fire. All through the game I was burning up. Worse was to come when I discarded the kit and entered the showers. It was unbearable. I looked over at Rollo who was blithely chatting away and working up a fine lather. Eventually I had to clean up and wash but even in the late evening in the pub I could feel this glow. I never ever used any kind of embrocation again.

My favourite story about Dave Rollo came from the Cardiff and Wales prop John Tess O' Shea, a man who liked a good scrap in the front row. Tess and I faced each other in a Barbarians v Cardiff game which was, to say the least, a bit tasty. At the end of the game we were chatting and I asked him if he had ever met anyone who had frightened him. He replied 'not really' but he had once played against this Scotsman who appeared with his socks around his ankles – a Rollo trademark. At that time people followed the ball into the scrum so Tess decided to kick his opponent instead of the ball. No reaction, so next scrum he repeated the dose whereupon a large mitt grabbed him by the throat followed by "I widnae dae that again pal."

O'Shea admitted that he did NOT bother to follow in again.

John Frame, Gala, played at three-quarters for Scotland more than twenty times coming in at the tail end of Dave's career. The following tale by him was related in *Behind the Thistle* published by Arena Sport.

Davie could be as fierce as he wanted to be, but he did his talking through his strength in the front-row. During our centenary season, Gala was asked to go to Howe of Fife for an exhibition match to open their new stand, and Davie was brought out of retirement to play the game. Gala was winning quite comfortably and it was a great day with beautiful weather and the ball was being thrown around by both sides.

Gala had this young prop – who I won't name so as to spare his blushes – and he had obviously decided that he was going to make his reputation against this old-stager from Fife. So he was pushing and pulling, and ducking and bucking. Davie just stood there like the man mountain he was.

At half-time, a very embarrassed and shy Mr Rollo came up to me and said, 'Hey John, can I have a word with your young prop?' I replied, 'Be my guest.'

And with the crowd all craning to see what was going on, he asked the boys to pack down, and he said, 'Now son, what you're trying to do is this, but you should be doing that. Drop your left shoulder here, and get your right foot back there.' This was at half-time and he was giving this boy in the opposing team a coaching lesson.

That was typical of Davie; while others might see psychological warfare in that, he genuinely wanted to help this boy who was getting it all wrong. He was a different breed.

Ian Kirkhope has been a stalwart of the Howe of Fife Rugby Club for more than fifty years. In his playing career, he was a versatile and talented forward who could, and did, play either as flanker or in the second row. He played alongside Dave in the North Midlands team

on a number of occasions as well as being a colleague in one of the best 'sevens' team the Howe have ever produced.

As a schoolboy in the early sixties, having just engaged with the sport of rugby football, I soon learned that the legend that is DMD, a lion of the 1960 tour to South Africa was a local celebrity and so with others took every opportunity to see our hero in action.

To begin with, trips to Murrayfield were the obvious choice, not only for the excitement of an international spectacle but also to see Dave in the flesh. Although he played at that time for his beloved Howe, his appearances for his local team were rare due to other rarefied rugby commitments.

In the mid-sixties a number of us rugby daft schoolboys would play on Saturday afternoons at Duffus Park for the lower XVs of the Howe. This opportunity allowed us to become acquainted with the darker arts of the game and the social interaction with senior players was of great personal benefit in future years. At this time DMD was viewed as a God to be watched in awe for his strength and physique but no verbal or social interaction. This rapidly changed, however, on leaving school.

I quickly became a team-mate of the great man, and was most fortunate and appreciative to have my hero as a mentor. Dave led by example, a man of few words, but some expletives. Although he took no prisoners, he was seen as a perfect gentleman both on and off the field. Dignity and modesty were shown at every level, being quite prepared to coach an opposite number provided they took no liberties, which would be fatal for them.

After forty international caps Dave continued to play District rugby and indeed had more time to boost the ranks at Howe. Regular appearances for the first XV improved morale and performance overall, leading to a number of seasons where the Howe of Fife RFC was seen as one of the best teams in the land. I was privileged to be part of this team.

As a youngster, one of my outstanding memories of the genuine regard his fellow international team mates had for him came after a humiliating defeat at Hawick by the South of Scotland. This was my first appearance for the North Midlands. The captain of Scotland, Peter Brown was approached by Dave to commiserate with me and offer advice on future performance. As a result of Dave's intervention Peter Brown led me to a table for two where we remained for the meal and indulged in rugby conversation far beyond my expectations. Surely a memory all young aspiring rugby players would only dream about.

There are so many rugby memories that I could allude to with regard to my now good friend David Rollo, possibly some he would not want to be in print or be reminded of. One thing is for sure, there could not have been a better role model and I sincerely thank him for that.

Kynoch Todd is a former captain of the Howe and a second row regular in the team behind Dave in the scrum. A pig farmer, he gained a certain notoriety in his playing days when asked to bring along a prize for a raffle at a Howe dance. He appeared with a live pig which then escaped from his grasp causing much confusion on the dance floor.

I played behind David in the second row for quite a long time, and when he was absent on international and district duties I had to work very hard to help my substitute prop. When he was present he used to say, "Just get doon there and hud me." What a joy that was for me. He was so strong. When the ball came in against the head he was able to stand on his left leg and help hook the ball with his right leg. Through doing so, he made two international hookers, Frank Laidlaw and Norman Bruce look good because they took so many balls against the head. They both admitted to me that he was the best prop for gaining the ball against the head and that was a big plus.

Along with Joe Manson – another Howe captain – I introduced Dave to golf, a sport in which he would have been a greater player if he had had more fire about him. It was always, "Come on boys that will do."

We made several trips to Edinburgh golf courses. He was going along not too badly but at one point I lost the head and slammed my club on the ground. I never thought much about it but Dave just said, "Now, now, keep the heid, keep the heid." By the second last hole, he was really getting into his game when he missed a putt from about two feet. He had his putter in his hand and he began swinging it round his head. He was going to throw it away. I just said, "Dave, keep the heid."

Another Howe player from farming stock, Alec Nicol played as hooker in the same North Midlands District team with Dave and recalls a pre match moment.
We were in the changing rooms getting ready for the match and I remember looking up at one point. The sun was glinting through the window and all I saw was Dave's heavily muscled profile outlined. I was glad he was alongside me and not against me.

One of the 2007 Bell Baxter school/Howe Scottish Youth Club champions and current Scottish international, Peter Horne recalls Dave's support for the young players coming through.
He was an inspiration for us boys knowing he had played for Scotland and for the Lions. Coming from a small club it is sometimes hard to imagine reaching the top but having Dave there was proof it can happen. He was always on the sidelines offering advice.

Brian Henderson played as a three-quarter alongside Dave in the Scottish team in a dozen internationals. He was in the same Scottish touring team that visited Canada in the early 1960s.
Part of our extra-curricular activities was to go round various schools to spread the rugby gospel. Dave and I were sent to a school in Ontario to

chat to the interested schoolboys. We were driven there by one of our hosts who found out that Dave was a farmer. He asked Dave where his farm was. Dave's response was "You have probably never heard of Wester Forret but it is quite near Cupar.' I think if Dave had just said Scotland, or even perhaps just Europe, it might have been a rough enough guide for our host to zero in on, so sparse was his knowledge of the Kingdom of Fife. 'And where about is Cupar, Mr Rollo?' he asked pronouncing Cupar as 'Queuepar' and Rollo as rhyming with hollow. 'It is in Fife,' explained Dave to a still confused Canadian.

One of the 1962 Lions, Bill Mulcahy, was a lock forward who from his Leinster club went on to play thirty five times for Ireland. His friendship with Dave now goes back more than fifty years.

On the Lions tour on one occasion I was sharing a room on the first floor with Dave in a hotel with a big veranda all around. Behind the bedroom door there was this fan light which was wide open for air. With great optimism the Prince (Dave) had left his heavy brogues outside the door in the hope that they might be polished for him. That used to be a tradition. I was fast asleep in the middle of the night when this brogue came through the fan light and hit me bang on the forehead giving me a nice little gash. Team mates who were coming back from a visit to the wine district and who shall be nameless, hurled the brogue through the fan light and it landed on my forehead.

Before one of the Test matches we had a break and the options were either to go to a hunt in the middle of some forest area or to go on a boat for deep sea fishing. I chose to go to the forest area. Dave went on the boat where he was strapped into the chair ready to do a bit of tuna fishing. Things were quiet in the fishing department and, I am told, he dozed off. Willie John McBride (another of the Lions) hauled in the line and tied a bucket to the end of it and threw it back overboard. The Prince woke up and began to tug on the line thinking he was pulling

Dave with his great Irish friend Bill Mulcahy.

in this bloody great big fish only to find he had landed a bucket of sea water.

When we played in Pretoria, I remember Dave and a handful of us getting on the team bus and, with no driver in sight, Dave sat behind the wheel of the bus and drove us through the streets of Pretoria safely back to our hotel.

Over the past fifty and more years Grant Robertson has been a member of the Howe of Fife. He has been everything from a player to president and from the bar manager to builder – along with his business partner, Jim Smart – of the original grandstand. He recalls Dave's relationship with team buses.

When Dave was president, he was a stickler for the team bus leaving on the appointed hour. One Saturday in Aberdeen, he had decided that the departure would take place at ten o'clock. Despite the bus being only half full at the time determined, he told the driver to head back to Fife. This left a number of Howe players – including one just home from his honeymoon - overnight in the Granite City.

Another prompt departure, this time from Stirling, saw several tardy members initially catching up with the bus and then hanging onto it as it gathered speed with the bus driver obeying instructions from Dave to 'carry on.'

Pat Melville played flanker in the same era as Dave and after their playing careers were over, both coached the youth and schoolboy teams. Dave also worked with Pat after his own farm had been sold. I played with Dave for seven or eight years. During part of that time he was club captain. He was a great figurehead.

Also during that time, the Howe organised a trip to Ireland where we played Coleraine and Ballymena. After the Ballymena game we stayed in a hotel in Portstewart. The team went out to a local dance and Dave and I stayed in the bar chatting to this big Irish farmer we had met. The team came back with Miss Ulster whom they had chanced upon and plonked her down between Dave and the Irishman. As if it had been choreographed, they both put their big rough farmers' hands on her knee. The look on the girl's face was one of horror as she jumped up and left. Dave looked across at the farmer and said, 'She left in a bit of a hurry.'

Dave and I were among the Howe members who started up coaching youngsters after the school PE teachers stopped taking sport on a Saturday.

Following coaching sessions we used to discuss matters. One day, Dave said to me that I was awfully hard on the boys. I replied that I just told them what I would have said on the farm. At the next game, one guy tried to catch the ball but knocked it on and it fell to the ground.

Dave went over and said to him, 'What are you doing down there, you big fat pudden?'

Another Howe stalwart who has served the club from player to president, Joe Manson remembers a few stories about Dave as well as a few of his sayings. In the mid-sixties, when first and second XVs travelled together on away fixtures, Howe spent a convivial evening in a hostelry named The Edge Lodge outside Glasgow.

We were back on the bus heading for home when we were stopped by the police who announced that the commissionaire's hat had been borrowed by a Howe member. Dave calmly stated, 'My boys wouldn't do a thing like that.' This seemed to satisfy the police and we were allowed to proceed homewards. A few miles further up the road a player came walking down the bus aisle wearing the missing hat. 'You b*gger,' said Dave with a smile.

There is much use of ice baths in the modern game for curing injuries and reducing swellings. Dave's method for dealing with such problems was to sit for hours on end with his leg in the burn which ran through the farm.

On one training night during Dave's international career a few of us turned up at Duffus Park to find the pitch covered with six inches of snow. Determined not to miss out on training, he drove his car round the pitch and we trained running around in the wheel tracks.

One of the legends of Irish rugby, Syd Miller from Ballymena, played for Ireland forty six times. Over two decades he played for, coached and managed the Lions. One of his early trips was the 1962 tour of South Africa with Dave as a team mate.

Dave was a very, very good player. He was much more than a strong prop, he was a good footballer. He was a great tourist both on and off the field.

Back in the late 1960s Ballymena (Syd's club) held an invitation game annually against top opposition. After the 1968 Lions tour, we invited a lot of the team and we added top players such as Dave. Players' wives were invited over as well and we put them all up in this hotel which did not have en-suite facilities. The Lions captain Tom Kiernan and his wife were asleep in bed when she nudged her husband in the ribs saying, 'There is a naked man trying to get into bed beside me.' It was the Prince. He had gone out for a widdle and lost his bearings.

Reunion in Dublin 2015. Left to right – Dave, Ronnie Dawson and Syd Miller.

Apart from playing in the Howe second row behind Dave, Andrew Adamson was a friend, neighbour and travelling companion. He was also Dave's best man.

With Dave in front, you could tell his strength, with the forwards often setting the base for the team winning. He was a pleasure to play alongside. He was and is always good and gentle company and we got up to quite a few high jinks on trips abroad.

He was very much in the amateur era. Today's top competitors would be amazed at how international players were treated.

*

In his twenty five years as a player, Dave Rollo competed against a multitude of other members of the 'front row mafia'. These are the strong men who are skilled in the skulduggery that can occur but who also enjoy the comradeship that exists between those who compete in the front line of action.

Dave made the following comments on a few of his colleagues and opponents.

The first prop I came across was **Bill Steven** who played for the Howe. He was a farmer from Auchtermuchty and whose nickname was 'the beast'. When it was a wet day Bill always put the ball down at his feet. That was the old traditional way to make a bit of ground. The forwards didn't carry the ball. They dropped it at their feet and dribbled it forward. I tried it a few times but I couldn't do it at all.

Bob Steven and **John Steven** were cousins of Bill and they came from a farm, Lawhill Craig, Largo. Both played for the Howe. Both joined Edinburgh Wanderers when they moved through to Edinburgh. John got into the trials, the final trials and Bob was awarded a cap when he took my place for the Irish game in 1964.

Then there were cousins **Chuck Hay** from Perthshire who went on to win the World Cup at curling, and his cousin **Jock Hay** who played for Panmure. I had a job holding my own against Chuck. Jock who was older than me was probably one of the toughest prop forwards I came across at the time. He must have thought I am going to teach this young pup a lesson or two about heeling the ball against the head. Instead of trying to follow the ball he stuck the front of his feet up so I was kicking the studs on his boots. I learned I had to get in a bit quicker.

Gordon Hill and **Ian Spence** both came from Gordonians and both played for the North Midlands. They were very good props. The Howe played against Gordonians twice a year in those days and we also met up for the District matches.

Bob Munro, from Leith Accies should have had a cap. He was probably about the best prop that I had played against up until that time (late 1950s). Leith Accies was a club at a lower level and I think he didn't get the chance he should have done.

Ian Hastie, Kelso, was one of the best props I have played against.

When we played in my final Scottish trial in 1968, **Ian McLauchlan**, Jordanhill College and Scotland, was the strongest prop I had played against my whole career.

The front row of the 1960s Springboks team, **Fanie Kuhn**, **Abie Malan** and **Piet De Toit** were all muscle and they were tough, very tough.

CHAPTER TEN

ROLLO REFLECTIONS

IN AUGUST 2016, Dave Rollo, as one of four former Howe of Fife players who went on to represent Scotland at rugby, was awarded the honour of cutting the ribbon to open the new clubhouse on the Duffus Park pitch.

The million pound plus investment with multiple changing rooms, meeting and catering facilities which overlooks a pitch with floodlights is a far, far cry from the very basic support Dave had sixty years earlier when he first turned out for the club. At the opening ceremony, Dave recalled his schoolboy days when he collected stones off the pitches, converting a farmer's field into a playing surface. He remembered his early days with the Howe when, after a match with no changing facilities on site, the teams would troop the mile or so down through Cupar in their muddy gear to wash and change in one of the bedrooms at the Royal Hotel.

From that inauspicious start in the mid-1950s, the club decided to establish its own pavilion on the Duffus Park site. This was opened at the start of the 1958/9 season with a game in which Dave played against Hawick who, at that time, were the giants of club rugby. It was at this match when the visitors won by sixteen points to three that Dave first came in close contact with the legendary Hughie McLeod. While on opposite sides on that occasion and in subsequent district matches between the North Midlands and the South of Scotland, the pair of props went on to form, in the opinion of many noted rugby writers, two-thirds of one of the best front rows Scotland has ever produced.

The original changing rooms on the Duffus Park were the first property owned by the Howe of Fife but, in 1967, they bought and converted a building in Provost Wynd in the centre of Cupar which had had a fairly chequered history as a chip shop, snooker hall and, some alleged, a dosshouse. Dave, the club captain at the time, was heavily involved in the conversion which required a great deal of clearing out of rubbish accumulated over the years from its various previous uses. He, and his colleagues then running the club, converted it into a clubhouse which was for many years thereafter a popular meeting place for visiting teams. The first visitors to the new premises came from another of the big Border teams – Melrose. They had been invited to play the Howe prior to the opening of the club's new home. These two significant games in the club's history also bore out a belief held by Dave throughout his career; that the best way of improving the game of rugby in clubs like the Howe was playing against the 'big boys' from the South of Scotland and the cities of Edinburgh and Glasgow.

Part of the interior décor – doors and wooden fittings – for the clubrooms in Provost Wynd came from the *Queen of Bermuda*. This was not a royal handout. It was merely because the ship of that name was being broken up in Faslane. President, Jimmy Gray, Dave and other club members decided some of the discarded furnishings would do nicely in Cupar.

A few years later, with his international career over, Dave then added a major and, possibly unique in rugby terms, contribution of his own to the clubhouse – his international jerseys. The collection included the bright red Lions top, plus one from each of the Home Countries. To these were added tops from South Africa, New Zealand, Australia, Canada and France. A distinctive Barbarians jersey completed this remarkable collection which was displayed in the clubhouse until its latest move to the new Duffus Park facility. There, Dave's jerseys are on show along with other memorabilia belonging to the club.

This latter collection includes a miner's helmet which marks the link between the Howe and Penygraig in the Rhondda Valley which started

Presentation of the international jerseys. L to R: Dave, Jean,
mother Nan and Ian Stewart, Howe president.

in the late 1950s. The Scottish/Welsh club connection was linked to
the international between the two countries being played. When the
game was played in Scotland droves of red shirted, leek sprouting,
anthem singing Welshmen descended on Cupar. Every other year, bus
and car loads of Howe members headed first to the valleys to play,
then on to Cardiff to support Dave and his Scottish team mates in
the international. Although the club fixture has now slipped off the
calendar, there are still friendships between Fife and the Rhondda
forged by this association.

Dave's tour of official duty with the Howe was completed in 1981
when he was elected club president. Confirming the family link to
the club his secretary at that time was his cousin, Bruce. Dave's uncle,
Landall was an office-bearer in the earlier years of the club.

The new premises sited by the side of the first fifteen pitch, give Dave and the rest of the supporters the opportunity to combine watching the games being played with social meetings before and after matches with his old colleagues.

Dave sits in the same seat at every home game and around him are his friends. Just as during his playing days, he seldom raises his voice but, when he does, it is most often issuing words of advice rather than complaint. Rowdier elements in the crowd who whistle and try to put the opposition goal kicker off are told quietly, but firmly, to desist. An "Enough of that," from him is sufficient to quell the unsportsmanlike behaviour. Players seeing the proverbial red mist and raising their fists in anger against an opponent are told by a man who has seen all sorts of shenanigans in his own career to "calm down."

His approach raises the question – was he ever sent off in his lengthy playing career? His answer is firmly in the negative. "Never, although one referee mistook my hand-off as a rabbit punch and threatened to send me off if I repeated it."

When Dave started playing, he was given a rule book and he used to read it two or three times a season to check out what was permitted and what was not. If there is a flare up or some dirty work in today's games, he believes much of the blame lies with the coaches. "The coaches study the opposition and they tell their own players maybe just to try and see if they could needle their opposite number a bit to see if he loses the plot. I am sure they have a lot to do with any bad behaviour on the field."

After matches, he catches up with old colleagues and they discuss the changes in the game from their day and it is soon clear Dave is no fan of modern day scrummaging; a part of the game where he was master. "To me nowadays there is no technique in what they are doing in the front row. It is just brute strength. There is no skill. The way the props are standing, the hooker can't even lift his leg to hook the ball. They are more or less nodding it back with their head. I can see the scrum going the same way as in rugby league where it is a case of 'It's your put in. You get the ball.'"

Dave believes the root cause of the present scrummaging problem lies in the training sledges; an innovation which came along only after he had gained his experience through man to man combat in the front row. "It is just man against machine. The front row go in there pushing against the pads and the pads are static. The pads are not moving up or down like human opposition when somebody could be pulling you down or trying to lift you up. The players are getting bigger and heavier and this means the coaches put more weight on the sledge. There is no skill. It is pure weight."

He would like to see the future of the sport being fifteen man rugby with the ball moving from the forwards to the three-quarters and back again. That is the game he played and that mobility of play involving all members of the team was one reason why he enjoyed playing for teams like the Barbarians who he once said, played "champagne rugby."

"That is what the spectators want to see," he claims.

With his playing career firmly in the amateur era – there was shock when one of the 1962 squad of Lions, Ronnie Cowan went off to play rugby league for money – Dave has strong and not always complimentary views on professional rugby. "I find, despite professionals being full time on the job, they make quite a lot of mistakes. Poor passing of the ball often lets them down. When they get the ball, they should not have to juggle it about first and when they go into a maul or loose scrum, they do not need to cuddle it. They should pass it out."

Dave's own link with professional rugby was brief almost to the point of non-existence. Following the Scotland versus France international in 1968 when he was a travelling reserve, Dave and one or two other Scots were invited up to one of the French official's hotel rooms. There they were offered the chance of playing for one of the French sides. This was no spur of the moment offer as the deal included accommodation in France for Jean and daughter Pat and it was targeted at players with specific skills. "They wanted strong mobile props," Dave recalled. However, he was 34 years old at the time and he decided his body could not take the pressure. Without even discussing cash, he left the room and he closed the door on his opportunity to play professional rugby.

He still follows the Scottish team. Often this is from his own armchair but in recent years he and Pat have travelled to Paris, Twickenham and Dublin to see the current Scottish team. Although half a century has passed since he pulled on a Scottish jersey, he is still recognised both by other former international players and by rugby enthusiasts. Post-match conversations with former opposition players are laced with anecdotes about their time in the public eye and of escapades out of the public gaze.

In his playing days, he had to rush back from rugby matches in order to catch up with work on the farm. That rush is no longer necessary as Dave and his brother moved out of the farm in 1985. This came about after the landlord wanted to increase the rent and Ian was thinking about retirement. The lease for the farm allowed the tenancy to be passed down to the next generation but neither Pat nor her cousins – Ian's son and daughter – wanted to go into farming. The decision was taken to cash in the lease allowing the landlord to take over the farm.

Preparing for the farm sale. L to R: Tom and Ann Balfour, Jyn (dog), Pat, Dave and Ian.

The roup or sale of all the farm machinery and livestock was held on 6th November 1985. Prior to the sale, all the big equipment was lined up in the small field beside the farm buildings. This allowed potential buyers to walk up and down the lines on the day of the sale.

The roup opened, as is the tradition, with small tools, such as spades, brushes, plough parts, hammers and all the other pieces of equipment needed to run a farm. In the Rollos' sale, because they had been in the farm for more than half a century and because Dave was a bit of a hoarder, there were hundreds of lots for auctioneer, Jimmy Weir to sell. What made this slightly easier was the desire of farming friends to get on the 'roup roll' or sale sheet; this being the custom of helping a colleague moving out of the industry. When that part was completed, the hundreds of fellow farmers, neighbours, dealers and just plain curious people following the auctioneer moved to the sale of the cattle and thereafter out to the field. A roup is both a work and a social occasion and when all the deals were done, Dave was swamped by people coming up to him to reminisce about the old days.

That was wonderful but all the while parts of his and his brother's business were being loaded on to lorries and trucks and being driven away. Next morning, Dave recalled seeing the empty farm buildings and thinking how horrible the bareness and quiet was after a lifetime when it had been a bustling business.

He and Jean moved to a small property near Dairsie where they kept a few sheep and Jean's ponies. For the next twenty years, Dave helped a farming friend and fellow rugby player, Pat Melville at busy spring and harvest times.

However by 2015, another move was on the cards when Dave and Jean moved into Cupar. This necessitated another sale as Dave had, in the intervening two decades, gathered a great deal of memorabilia and some vintage farm machinery, none of which could be accommodated in their retirement home. Hundreds of lots were sold that day with the top price being gained for a 1962 Fordson Super Major which Dave had

Dave & Jean in retirement

bought for £400. The bidding was brisk before it was knocked down for £2,500.

In pride of place in their new Cupar abode is a trophy cabinet. This contains a small blue velvet skull cap with silver braid, a tassel and a thistle emblem. Despite its now rather faded appearance, this is the 'Scottish Cap' presented to those chosen to represent their country. Dave had to get his head measured for this prestigious item of apparel at a famous outfitters in Edinburgh prior to his first game for Scotland. While his nephews have on occasion put on 'the Cap' when visiting their uncle, Dave has never been asked to wear this little cap with the date of his first international – 1959 – marked on the peak. Dave recalls that his old colleague, Hughie McLeod decided to add later dates to his single Cap but ran out of space before his retiral.

Tucked away below the display cabinet are bundles of scrapbooks which Jean lovingly filled with all the newspaper comments about Dave throughout his international career. These contain the highlights of his lengthy period as a player. The bare facts are: he represented his country forty times – then a record but now, with far more internationals being played, superseded by players with more than one hundred caps. Of the forty games, Dave was on the winning side on sixteen occasions and drew five times. His best record is against the Irish whom he played seven times, in all bar one being on the winning side. He also had a 100% record against Australia but, he admits, that signifies one out of one played. Three wins against England and Wales and two against France complete his winning tally.

And what does he think now? "I was lucky," and when reminded of golf legend, Gary Player's maxim that the harder he worked, the luckier he became, Dave modestly dismisses that suggestion.

He is a modest man but he has an enviable record. He is a local hero.

ABOUT THE AUTHOR

Andrew Arbuckle was brought up on a farm in North Fife and after farming until the mid 1980s, he devoted his time to writing. Currently, he is Farming Editor of the *Scotsman*. He has two daughters and this book is dedicated to his three grandchildren.

ALSO BY THE SAME AUTHOR

Footsteps in the Furrow – a social history of farming in twentieth century Scotland

We Waved to the Baker – a collection of schoolboy tales from the 1950s

The First One Hundred Years – a history of NFU Scotland

Sparks from the Smiddy – the life story of David Wilson, world champion blacksmith

Farming is a Funny Business – a collection of jokes and anecdotes from farming